NEVADA CITY

For Fred —
Historian & Railroader

With Best Wishes,

Orval Bronson
Nevada City
Sept 26, 2002

Lower Broad Street, looking east, in 1857

NEVADA CITY

Orval Bronson

NEVADA COUNTY HISTORICAL SOCIETY
NEVADA CITY, CALIFORNIA

Published by Nevada County Historical Society, Inc.
P. O. Box 1300, Nevada City, CA 95959-1300

NORTHERN MINES SERIES

ISBN 0-915641-11-9 (Hardcover limited edition)
ISBN 0-915641-12-7 (Trade paperback)

Design, composition and production by David Comstock

ILLUSTRATION CREDITS

All illustrations are from the archival collections of the Searls
   Historical Library at Nevada City, with these exceptions:

Institutions

California Historical Society, San Francisco, CA—p. 15.

California State Library, Sacramento, CA—pp. 7, 19, 20, and 49.

Comstock Bonanza Press, Grass Valley, CA—pp. 10, 11, 14, 17,
   21, 27, 29, 31, 32, 36, 40, 41, 46 (left), 47, 52, 55, 57, 63, 77, 78
   (left), 79 (top left), and 83.

Los Angeles Times, Los Angeles, CA—p. 62 (bottom).

Photographers

© 2002 Gay Conner, Grass Valley, CA—Front cover; pp. 46
   (right), and 65.

© 2002 Robert M. Wyckoff, Nevada City, CA—p. 48 (bottom).

This book is dedicated to those local history
preservationists who have gone before
and have left a wealth of information
for those who follow.

Acknowledgments

My grateful thanks to David Comstock and Edwin Tyson for their content assistance and editing skills, and to Wallace Hagaman, Steve Cottrell, Gary Stollery, Maria Brower, Allan Rogers, Leo La Brie, Madeline Helling and Nevada City City Manager Beryl Robinson Jr. for their contributions. I am also indebted to the staffs of the Searls and Doris Foley historical libraries and to the staff of the Nevada City office of the Tahoe National Forest.

Contents

List of Illustrations

Photographs and Drawings

Maps

Nevada City Timeline

January 24, 1848	James Marshall discovers gold at Coloma
February 2, 1848	With signing of Treaty at Guadalupe Hildago, Mexico cedes California and New Mexico territories to U. S.
July 30, 1849	Charles Marsh at confluence of Gold Run Creek and Deer Creek
Sept. 1849	John Pennington, Thomas Cross and William McCaig built cabin at confluence of Gold Run Creek and Deer Creek
October 1849	A. B. Caldwell opened his "upper store" at Gold Run-Deer Creek.
February 18, 1850	California split into 27 counties; Yuba County included present- day Yuba, Sierra, Nevada and parts of Placer and Butte Counties; Marysville was county seat
April 17, 1850	Originally called "Deer Creek Dry Diggings" and "Caldwell's Upper Store," present-day Nevada City was named "Nevada"
July 1850	First religious society (non-denominational) organized; church built on Main Street
September 9, 1850	California admitted to the Union as a free state
March 11, 1851	125 homes, stores, hotels and saloons destroyed by fire
March 13, 1851	Nevada incorporated by legislative act. Town soon called Nevada City
April 19, 1851	First newspaper (*Nevada Journal*) established
May 18, 1851	Governor signed bill establishing Nevada County. Boundaries redrawn with Nevada City as county seat
June 8, 1851	Hamlet Davis opened first theater (Dramatic Hall) on second story of his store at Broad and Pine Streets

November 20, 1851	Jenny Lind Theater opened; built over Deer Creek on Main Street, it was destroyed by major storm on March 3, 1852
February 14, 1852	Legislature repealed Nevada City charter at request of citizens
September 7, 1852	12 buildings at the Plaza destroyed by fire
November 1853	First brick building completed on Broad Street
September 1853	Concert Hall built on Washington (Coyote) Street
October 5, 1853	Telegraph line installed, connecting Nevada City to Sacramento
1853	Piped water supplied to homes and businesses
1853	Nevada City again incorporated
November 28, 1854	Nine buildings on Main Street destroyed by fire
February 20, 1855	15 buildings on Broad Street destroyed by fire
April 19, 1856	Law under which Nevada City incorporated ruled unconstitutional
April 19, 1856	Nevada City again incorporated; now 3rd largest town in California, behind San Francisco and Sacramento
July 19, 1856	Most of town destroyed by fire
February 1857	Disastrous flood resulting from Laird's Dam collapse carried off bridges on Main and Broad streets and several businesses
May 23, 1858	200 wood buildings in business section of town destroyed by fire; 30 brick buildings survived
1859	Miners Foundry built on Spring Street
June 12, 1860	Fire Company Number One formed
June 13, 1860	Fire Company Number Two formed
July 7, 1860	Charles Marsh awarded contract to supply water to Nevada City
June 1862	Pine Street suspension bridge completed
July 11,1862	Pine Street bridge gave way, killing 2 men and 15 oxen
November 14, 1862	Pine street bridge reopened

November 8, 1863	Fire destroyed downtown business section, the courthouse and all churches except the Baptist; the Union and National Exchange Hotels were rebuilt in 1864
1869	U.S. Patent granted for 644.68 acres for Nevada City
May 21, 1876	Nevada County Narrow Gauge Railroad began service between Nevada City, Grass Valley and Colfax
March 12, 1878	Nevada City again incorporated by legislative act
1880	Fire destroyed Chinatown
October 15, 1901	Nevada County Traction Co. began regular electric trolley service between Nevada City and Grass Valley
April 4, 1902	Nevada City Chamber of Commerce formed
1904	Pine Street bridge rebuilt
October 1905	Pacific Gas and Electric Company formed at National Hotel
January 3, 1924	Electric trolley service discontinued
June 19, 1937	Works Progress Administration completed construction of city hall on Broad Street
April 4, 1938	Narrow gauge passenger service discontinued
July 10, 1942	Last narrow gauge revenue train ran
1942-1945	Federal government closed mines during WWII
1967-1970	Golden Center freeway (State Highway 49/20) opened
August 12, 1968	Historical Ordinance enacted
1978	Downtown Betterment Project
1996	Pine Street bridge rebuilt
December 19, 2000	City Hall renovation completed

Introduction

In 1834 Bavarian-born, Swiss-raised John Sutter, plagued by debt and facing debtor's prison, left his family and sailed to New York. Heading west in 1836, Sutter arrived in Monterey in 1839 and met with Mexican Governor Juan Alvarado, telling Alvarado of his plans to develop a colony for migrating Swiss and other Europeans. Alvarado, reportedly having difficulty with the Nisenan (the southern branch of the Maidu Indian tribe), saw an advantage in having an outpost in the northern valley and gave Sutter permission to explore the area and to take eleven Spanish leagues (76 square miles) of his choosing for his outpost.

Sutter sailed up the Sacramento River and made port at the confluence of the Sacramento and American Rivers; he built his compound nearby, which still stands at its original location, now Sutter's Fort State Historical Park. Sutter's grant was finalized by Alvarado in June 1841, as was his status as a Mexican citizen that was required as a condition of the land grant.

By 1844 New Helvetia, as Sutter had named his compound, was a stable outpost and immigrant refuge. As more people settled in the area the Mexicans became concerned that their authority was being diluted. About the same time, the United States government concluded that it was not going to be denied access to the Pacific—President Polk had made California's annexation to the Union a priority of his administration.

The Mexican-American war started in Texas when Mexican troops crossed the Rio Grande River on April 25, 1846, and attacked and killed several Americans. On May 13, 1846 President Polk declared the United States to be at war with Mexico. Although the war spread to California, northern California (primarily Yerba Buena and Monterey) was taken by the Americans without bloodshed, as the Mexicans had no ammunition or other supplies with which to put up any significant resistance. Battles that took place in southern California were concluded relatively quickly. The war ended in January 1847 but it was not until February 1848 that Mexico, via the Treaty of Guadalupe Hidalgo, ceded the California and New Mexico territories to the United States.

California, governed after the war by the military, was in disarray. Unpaid, discharged soldiers wandered the streets of the cities. There was no civil law and few sanctions for criminal activity. Additionally, Mexican land grants, particularly those of Pio Pico (the last Mexican governor) were poorly drawn and could not be legally perfected. Until statehood, there were no constitutional guarantees and none of the amenities associated with a progressive society, e.g., roads, schools and libraries. With seemingly disinterested military administrators coming and going frequently, there was little continuity or social order.

A constitutional convention was called in Monterey in 1848 wherein documents for a state constitution were assembled and a state government was formed. In 1849 there was a governor and legislature with a constitution, but no state until September 9, 1850, when Congress authorized California's admission to the Union as a free state.

It was during these unsettled times that Sutter sent employee James Marshall to the Sierra foothills to erect a sawmill. At Coloma, on January 24, 1848, Marshall discovered gold on the American River and by August 1848 there were in excess of 4000 gold seekers engaged in mining the rivers and streams of the Sierra foothills.

Argonauts thereafter came by the thousands, from the east by one of several overland routes, by ship around Cape Horn, across the Isthmus of Panama and from ports around the world.

California and the nation were never to be the same.

2

The Nisenan

The aboriginal inhabitants of Nevada City and environs were the *Nisenan*, one of three branches of the *Maidu* Indian language group. Also called the southern Maidu, the Nevada City area Indians were the "hill" Nisenan (as distinguished from the "valley" Nisenan, who inhabited the lower foothills and the Sacramento Valley). Other Maidu branches were the northwestern Maidu (also called the Konkow) who inhabited the Butte County area, and the northeastern Maidu in the Plumas County area.

The Nisenan socially and politically was made up of tribelets that consisted of one or more villages headed by one chief. Kin inhabited each village within the tribelet, and each dwelling within the village was occupied by a nuclear family. The permanent Nisenan villages were located below the snowline and were situated on a knoll, generally near a stream or spring. During the non-winter months, the villages were temporarily repositioned at higher elevations to take better advantage of hunting and fishing opportunities.

The Maidu were primarily hunters and gatherers. Hunting was the exclusive domain of men, while gathering (nuts, acorns, berries, etc.) was the domain of the women. The women also made baskets that were used as vessels, as the native northern California Indians did not make pottery.

Although generally peaceful, the Maidu were capable of aggression, occasionally going to battle over theft or trespass—the latter offense usually committed by the Washoe, who inhabited the eastern slope of the Sierra and who occasionally ventured into Maidu territory to hunt.

The primary tribelet in Nevada City consisted of three villages and was located in an area near the courthouse (current intersection of Pine and Church streets). The tribelet was referred to as the *Oustomah*, which according to one interpretation meant "near the town."

As the Nevada City area became inundated with gold-seekers, the Oustomah were pushed further out and relocated to

Charlie Cully (left) and Louie Kelly (above) were leaders of Oustomah village in the early twentieth century.

the Cement Hill area, a short distance northwest of Nevada City. The Nisenan encampment was called a "campoodie."

The hill Nisenan were reportedly unaffected by early nineteenth-century Spanish soldier-explorers who entered the Sacramento Valley looking for mission sites. North American and European trappers arrived in that same valley a decade or so later, bringing with them a disease generally thought to be malaria, which killed 20,000 valley Nisenan.

The culture and lifestyle of the hill Nisenan was forever changed by the gold rush. When the Nisenan resisted territorial invasion, theft of resources, or crimes against their persons, they were subjected to the white man's lynch laws. Local militia destroyed their villages, and some gold-seeking immigrants indiscriminately killed Nisenan adults and children.

In 1850 and 1851 several area tribelets signed treaties with the federal government. The Nisenan surrendered their lands in exchange for government protection, life-sustaining provisions and the promise of land to be set aside for reservations. These treaties were essentially the 1830 Indian Removal Act, extended as a result of the westward expansion policies of President Polk. Congress, however, refused to ratify the treaties, and by 1854 many Nisenan were homeless and starving.

With American Indians facing extinction, Congress passed

the Dawes Severalty Act in 1887 (commonly called the Allotment Act), which "gave" Indians who were not living on reservations individual 160-acre parcels of land. Hundreds of thousands of acres of former Indian land were then sold at bargain prices to whites. The Indian Removal Act, the Allotment Act, and government policies of Assimilation, Toleration and Termination (forced assimilation) were failures, and combined to displace and decimate the indigenous population.

The last of the Oustomahs at Nevada City were Betsy Westfield and Josie Cully. Betsy, grandmother of Louie Kelly (who became chief in 1919), was blind and was always accompanied by Josie, widow of former chief Charlie Cully. Betsy died in 1923 at age 105; Josie died in 1940 at age 90. Both were reportedly buried near their campoodie.

Blind Betsy Westfield (left) was the grandmother of Nisenan chief Louie Kelly. Her friend and constant companion, Josie Cully (right), was the widow of Charlie Cully, the former chief.

The First Arrivals

A t the time of the arrival of the first argonauts in the region that would ultimately be named Nevada City, California was not yet even an official territory of the United States, and there were no local political subdivisions or governments.

The first of the new arrivals was Charles Marsh in July 1849; John Pennington, Thomas Cross and William McCaig followed in September. All four prospected at Deer Creek, which skirts the east and south sides of Nevada City, and Gold Run, a stream that crosses under Sacramento Street, joining Deer Creek at the Pine Street bridge.

"Dr." A. B. Caldwell arrived in October and set up a miners supply store. The community was known as "Caldwell's upper store," or "Deer Creek Dry Diggings" until April 17, 1850, when locals desired a new name for their camp. Nevada—Spanish for "snow-covered"—was the preferred suggestion and was unanimously adopted.

Of the original arrivals only Charles Marsh had a continuing impact on the community (as well as the state and nation). He formed and developed a water company that supplied water to the gold mines and in 1860 supplied water through a piped system to the city, of Nevada; further, he supplied water free of charge for the purpose of fighting fires. Marsh's various water company ventures were the beginnings of what ultimately became the hydraulic division of Pacific Gas and Electric Company.

Marsh, with Theodore Judah, was also instrumental in the organization and routing of the Central Pacific Railroad through Colfax and over the summit. Both were on the first board of directors, along with notables Leland Stanford, Collis Huntington, Mark Hopkins and E. B. Crocker. Although he did not live to see its completion, Marsh was also a significant force in the organization and building of the Nevada County Narrow Gauge Railroad, which ran from Nevada City and Grass Valley to Colfax, where it connected with the Central Pacific Railroad.

Marsh's home at 123 Nevada Street (almost exactly on the earlier site of Caldwell's upper store) is one of the older homes

Placer miners operating sluices and long toms near Nevada City posed for a pioneer daguerreotypist in 1852.

in Nevada City, and is presently owned by the Nevada County Historical Society.

In February 1850 California was divided into 27 counties. Yuba County originally included present-day Yuba, Sierra, and Nevada counties, and parts of Placer and Butte counties. Marysville was designated the Yuba County seat.

On September 9, 1850, California was admitted to the union as a free state. By this time, the city of Nevada was growing, both in size and in prominence, and Marysville, the county seat, was too distant to be effective. In April 1851 the state legislature redivided the state and created several new counties, including Nevada County, named for its new county seat.

Early Government and the Judicial System

Government

In March 1850 the residents of Nevada City, recognizing that some form of government was becoming necessary, elected Mr. Stamps as *alcalde,* a judicial officer under Mexican law and most similar to a combined mayor and justice of the peace. On April 1, 1850, the *Court of Sessions* of Yuba County (of which Nevada City was then a part) ordered an election for *justice of the peace.* Albion N. Olney, an attorney and former Rhode Island secretary of state, was elected and served until John Edwards was elected to replace him in the October general election.

In the winter of 1850–1851 a charter was prepared for the incorporation of Nevada City. It was passed by the legislature on March 13, 1851, and Hamlet Davis was chosen *mayor* at a premature election. When it was discovered they had jumped the gun, another election was held on April 14, and Moses F. Hoit was elected legally. Nine *aldermen* were chosen and a city hall on Main Street was purchased. A jail was built and a lot and building for a hospital was purchased. However, city expenses became insurmountable and city operations were suspended. Upon petition the legislature repealed the city's charter in 1852.

Nevada City was again incorporated by the court of sessions in 1853 and in January 1854 an interim board of *town trustees* was elected. At the regular election in May of that year a new board was elected. The members were lumberman A. B. Gregory, James Harvey Helm (a partner in the Empire Livery Stable), and physician, pharmacist and newspaperman William G. Alban. Also elected to the board were jeweler Charles W. Young and George W. Dickinson. James C. Malbon, Alney O. Felt and John S. Foster were elected *marshal, treasurer* and *assessor* respectively.

In 1856 the state supreme court ruled that the law granting authority to the court of sessions to incorporate towns was unconstitutional. By legislative act Nevada City was again incor-

porated on April 19, 1856. In March 1863 Nevada City was surveyed and mapped by Ostram and Coswell.

In 1866 the city applied for a patent for 644.86 acres, the
land upon which the city was situated. (This land technically still
belonged to the federal government, which was about to give much
of it to the Central Pacific Railroad Company under terms of the
amended Pacific Railroad Act.) The patent was granted by the
United States in 1869, and Nevada City in turn provided lot-
owners with legal title to their individual properties.

Nevada City was again incorporated by legislative act on March
12, 1878. This city government consisted of five trustees, an assessor, a
marshal and a treasurer. On August
24, 1878, town trustees purchased
land with a building on Broad Street
and remodeled the building for use as
a city hall. It functioned as such until
1935, when it was demolished and a
new city hall was built on the same
site by the Works Progress Administration (WPA).

City Hall 1878–1935.

The Judicial System

The first California constitution, drawn in September 1849 at the
Constitutional Convention in Monterey, was ratified by voters in
the following month. The constitution, modeled after the federal
constitution and the state constitutions of Iowa and New York,
provided for the typical three branches of government and ar-
ticulated the hierarchy of the judiciary. The highest state court
was a three-justice *supreme court*; the lower court system consisted of *district, county* and *justice courts*.

In February 1850 California was split into 27 counties; Yuba
County, with Marysville as the county seat, included what is presently Nevada County as well as present-day Sierra County and
parts of Placer and Butte Counties. Yuba and Sutter counties
were placed in the Eighth Judicial District. *District courts*, which
generally had jurisdiction over areas encompassing more than
one county, had original jurisdiction in civil matters where the
amount in question exceed $200.00, in matters relating to prop-

The county's first brick courthouse was completed only days before the devastating 1856 fire burned the roof and gutted its interior. After it was restored the building burned again in the city-wide fire of 1863.

erty titles, validity of taxes, issues of fact in probate matters and criminal inquiry via the grand jury process.

In May 1851 California was redivided and Nevada County was formed. The creation of Nevada County and the designation of Nevada City as county seat necessitated accommodations for county officers, courts and prisoners. The first court was held in an existing structure located at Main and Church Streets, near the site of the present courthouse.

The county then purchased a building on Broad Street to use as a courthouse. A two-cell jail was constructed across the street from the courthouse that by 1854 became unusable due to general deterioration. Court was thereafter held variously at the Methodist and Congregational churches, Frisbie's Theatre and Abbott Hall.

The courthouse was completely redesigned after the 1863 fire and rebuilt on the same site overlooking Nevada City.

A third story was added to the courthouse in 1900.

The continuing need for an adequate courthouse led to the passage of a bill in the state legislature authorizing the issuance of bonds for the purpose of erecting a courthouse. The building was essentially completed when it was gutted in the fire of July 19, 1856. The structure was rebuilt by January 1857 and burned again on November 8, 1863. A new structure was completed in March 1865.

In the 1930s a slick art-deco facade was superimposed on the courthouse, with this startling result. After the passage of time, however, even this aberration is accepted with a sigh as one more bit of exotic patina for a gold rush monument.

In that same year the state supreme court took from the district courts original jurisdiction over criminal matters and conferred it on the *court of sessions*. The district courts, however, were left with authority to hear criminal appeals from the court of sessions and the power to try indictments for serious felonies.

The court of sessions, which also functioned as an administrative body, was composed of the county judge and two justices of the peace. The county judge also functioned as an appellate court for appeals from the justice courts. The first county judge in Nevada County was Thomas H. Caswell, who served in that capacity from 1851 to 1859. Caswell is also known for having written the Nevada County Rules of Court in 1856, rules which continue to be the basis of jurisprudence in California.

John R. McConnell was the first elected district attorney of Nevada County, serving from 1851 to 1853. At various times in practice with William M. Stewart and Addison C. Niles, McConnell was elected state attorney general in 1853. He was an unsuccessful Democratic candidate for governor of California in 1861, losing to Republican Leland Stanford, then president of the Central Pacific Railroad. Also on that ticket was Republican Aaron A. Sargent of Nevada City, who was successful in his bid to become a U. S. Congressman. McConnell left Nevada County in the 1870s and moved to southern California where he was elected to the state assembly from Los Angeles in 1875.

By legislative act, courts of session were abolished in 1863 and their duties taken over by newly-created *boards of supervisors*. The legislature also expanded the county court's authority by giving it original jurisdiction over all but the most serious felonies which had to be certified to the district court.

The provisions of a new state constitution, adopted in May 7, 1879, essentially abolished the district and county courts in favor of *superior courts*, which assumed the authority of both abolished courts. The new constitution also created justice courts and other inferior courts as necessary.

Mining

Placer Mining

The first miners in the Nevada City area who worked the rivers, streams and dry streambeds, as well as those who mined other areas of the Sierra drainage basin, used rudimentary tools—i.e. picks, shovels and pans—to retrieve gold. Placer mining, also known as surface mining, sometimes initially involved no more than picking up flakes or nuggets, or picking under rocks in the streambeds with a pocketknife. The pans were used to get water moving over the material thought to contain gold, washing away the lighter sand and sediment and leaving the heavier gold.

Owners of the larger valley land grants brought to their claims enslaved Indians or Mexican workers as a labor force. Other miners saw the advantage of large-scale operations and hired Indians for wages. To make their labors more efficient, miners without access to a labor force brought in "rockers" (also known as "cradles" because they resembled a child's cradle) used earlier in the gold mines of Georgia and North Carolina. The rocker, usually about 40 inches long and 20 inches wide, operated on the same principle as the gold pan, but was larger and utilized a screen to trap the gold as introduced water washed away the sediment.

Later in the first mining season came the "long tom"—usually 12–15 feet long—and "sluice boxes"—board flumes, cleated across the bottom and coated with mercury to catch and detain the gold. The largest sluices were primarily associated with hydraulic mining and were sometimes thousands of feet long. The pans, rockers, toms and sluices all served the same function—separating the gold from the sediment.

A placer mining claim, typically 100 square feet in productive areas, had to be "worked" one day per week for possession to be recognized (there was no ownership). When not present on the claim a tool was left in plain sight to signify possession. A miner could possess a maximum of two claims—one by discovery and one by purchase—at any given time.

PANNING OUT.

The above represents the primitive method of mining. A pan filled with earth is set into the water, and by shaking it from side to side, the dirt is washed out, and the gold gradually sinking to the bottom of the pan, is there saved. This method is still used by every company to wash out the product of the days' labor; while the Chilian or Mexican uses the pan or bowl exclusively.

ROCKING THE CRADLE.

The earth to be washed is carried in buckets to the cradle, and emptied into the seive or hopper, when water from a dipper is poured upon it; as the cradle is rocked from side to side, the earth and water falls through the seive upon an apron sloping towards the back of the cradle, and passing over the bottom, is washed out at the end — while the gold remains on the apron, or at the end of the cradle. Chinamen are the principal operators now with this machine.

SINKING A SHAFT

Is represented in the above engraving. These are sunk to ascertain if there is *pay dirt* upon the bed rock, or in any strata of gravel above it; or to find the basin or hollow in the rock upon a hill before commencing to tunnel. Sometimes all the pay dirt is thus hoisted by the windlass. These shafts are frequently very deep; one at Weaverville, Trinity Co., is 625 feet in depth.

GROUND SLUICING.

This illustrates one of the many methods of ground sluicing. A trench is first dug down the hill-side, into which a small stream of water is turned; miners then stand across or in the stream, and with their picks loosen the gravel and dirt, while the force of the water carries it into a sluice below. Sometimes a stream of water is made to run by the side of a bank, and by undermining or picking down the bank, it falls into the water, by which it is removed, and the pay dirt is afterwards carefully washed.

SLUICING.

To the right a company of miners are "sluicing;" those at the upper end are throwing in the pay dirt, and the man at the lower end is tending the sluice. Several lengths of sluice-boxes, or troughs with the ends out, supported by tressels, form the sluice; across the bottom, inside, are riffles or false bottoms, to save the gold; a stream of water being turned down, the gold is separated from the dirt, which is washed out

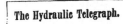

CANALS.

The above is intended to represent a Canal, by means of which the water of a river or creek, after winding among the hills for many miles, supplies the mining districts with water. They are built at great cost, and are a great public convenience, for without them the mines would be comparatively useless. The time may come when the whole of the water from our mountain streams will be needed for mining and manufacturing purposes, and will be sold at a price within the reach of all.

Hydraulic Washing.

The scene represents a company of miners washing down the hill by the Hydraulic process. The water from above being confined in a strong hose, is played through a pipe upon the bank of sand and gravel, with great force and effect. By this process, great quantities of earth are washed down, and passing through a long sluice, the gold is there saved. Sometimes where the gold is very fine, the Guyaskutus is of great value to the miner, saving nearly enough to pay his weekly water bill.

The Hydraulic Telegraph.

The above represents the manner of constructing the "Hydraulic Telegraph," as it is named. A small flume is placed upon poles or high tressels, through which the water is conveyed from the canal or ditch to a barrel or square wooden funnel at the end, to which is attached the hose. These Telegraphs are generally from 80 to 130 feet above the pipe from which the water escapes, thus creating the required force for washing down banks of earth into the sluice.

Mining techniques as described in 1857 by a California magazine.

14

Miners working their claim at Coyoteville in October 1850. E. D. Wadsworth (center front) washes paydirt in a tub while others operate a windlass to raise a bucket from bottom of their shaft.

The rivers, creeks and streams, while rich in gold, were shallow in yield and heavily burdened by thousands of arriving miners. As the yield lessened, the miners followed ravines up the hills to look for the source of the placer gold. Not being mining engineers or geologists, they were not aware that the source was the mountains themselves, that gold from the rivers and streams has been washed from the mountains by thousands of years of rain and flooding.

As the miners headed uphill, they came across gravel beds, the residual of ancient rivers, once part of the country's drainage system, now filled with quartz, granite, slate and other rocks of the Sierra. These gravel beds were mined by digging holes and removing the gold-laden material. Because the holes resembled those dug by coyotes, the mining process became known as "coyoting." The first of these gravel beds to be mined locally was in the northwest portion of what present-day Nevada City and gave rise to a community called Coyoteville, soon thereafter merely a suburb of Nevada City.

Material taken from the gravel beds (also known as "dry

diggings") had to be taken to a water source (river or stream) for washing. This process was not efficient and eventually a system of ditches and flumes was developed to bring water to the mining sites.

Quartz (Hardrock) Mining

In October 1850 a man thought to be George McKnight is reputed to have discovered gold-bearing quartz sticking out of the ground near what is now the intersection of Hocking and Jenkins streets in Grass Valley. During the same month, a ledge (a layer of quartz between ordinary rock) was discovered near Nevada City, and the visible quartz became the object of the first hardrock mining efforts in the area.

The placer miners were ill equipped to separate the gold-bearing quartz from the granite rock. They knocked off some outcroppings with hand drills and hammers, which they pulverized and then panned, but soon realized that these techniques would not be profitable. Miners banded together, mining companies were formed and capital was obtained through investors and the sale of stock so that mining could continue underground.

Cornish miners, learning of the transition from placer to hardrock mining, emigrated to California's goldfields armed with tin- and copper-mining experience, and intimate knowledge of drilling and blasting techniques. They also brought designs for a mining tunnel dewatering device (it became known in America as the "Cornish pump") and a primitive stamp mill (improved upon by the Californians and used for crushing small rock). The larger rock blasted from the hillsides was first crushed by one of two types of crushers, either the "jawbreaker" or the "gyrator breaker," into pieces no larger than two inches and then run through the stamp mill.

Pulverized by a stamp mill (an example of which can be seen in Nevada City at the foot of Main Street) the material was pushed through a screen and on to a sloped copper table. The table was coated with mercury that adhered to the gold; the gold was then separated from the mercury.

Hardrock mining (like hydraulic mining) requires enormous amounts of power to operate hoists, bring up ore carts from the mines, operate rock crushers and stamp mills and maintain machine shops. Although wooden water wheels of a type used in midwestern flour mills were tried, their design limited their power generation capabilities. Steam engines became the power source of choice but used wood as fuel which soon resulted in deforestation of the hills. Steam engines at Grass Valley's Empire Mine, for example, consumed about 20 cords of wood daily.

Iron waterwheels were developed and improved during the 1860s and 1870s, the most significant improvements being the replacement of paddles with cups and improvement of the water nozzle. This improved water wheel, about 65% efficient, was still thought to be of inadequate design by Lester Pelton of Camptonville. In 1878 Pelton perfected his wheel using a twin-cupped design, which he then had built at George G. Allan's foundry on Spring Street in Nevada City. Pelton's wheel tested at more than 90% efficiency.

The Pelton wheel, ranging in size from tiny 4-inch models used to power sewing and washing machines to the 30-foot model on display at the North Star Power House mining museum in Grass Valley, became the industry standard. A 12-foot model, displayed at the foot of Main Street in Nevada City, weighed 15 tons, developed 18,000 horsepower and provided enough power to light 16,000 homes.

The Pelton wheel depended on a sometimes unreliable water source and was somewhat supplanted by electricity in the 1880s

PELTON WATER WHEEL.

and 1890s. It continues, however, to power hydroelectric plants in California and throughout the world where water is plentiful.

Hydraulic Mining

Hydraulic mining involves pressurized water directed against a natural bank. The process was developed in 1853, in part as a response to the cave-in dangers inherent in hardrock mining and in part because it was a more efficient method of mining gold.

In 1852 Anthony Chabot, a French-Canadian later associated with public utility projects in Oakland, California, is generally thought to be the first miner to bring water to his coyote diggings instead of taking dirt to the water. Chabot fashioned a six-inch hose about 100 feet long by sewing together strips of canvas. Although there was no nozzle, there was some pressure that proved effective in separating the gold from the dirt.

A year later Edward E. Matteson of Nevada City is generally credited with the idea of breaking up a bank with pressurized water using the canvas hose, first with a tapered end and later with an attached nozzle. The process soon evolved from canvas hoses to 18-inch pipes of boiler iron and from tin nozzles to iron "cannons" or "monitors" with orifices up to 9 inches in diameter.

Although hydraulic mining continueed on a small scale in the Nevada City area, the largest and most productive operation was the Malakoff Mine, operated by the North Bloomfield Gravel Mining Company about 20 miles northeast of Nevada City. The state of California now incorporates the mine and buildings as Malakoff Diggins State Historic Park.

The hydraulicking process at the Malakoff Mine, which operated from 1853 to about 1884, required copious amounts of water and produced thousands of tons of debris daily. The mercury-tainted soil and mine tailings, carried by huge volumes of water, polluted streams and rivers and killed fish and other aquatic wildlife. The Sacramento and Yuba Rivers were rendered unnavigable for steamboats for several decades, and the town of Marysville and the agricultural areas of the Central Valley were subjected to severe flooding.

Years of individual lawsuits, some decided in favor of the farmers, others in favor of the miners, culminated in the Sawyer Decision, rendered in San Francisco in 1884 by federal judge Lorenzo Sawyer. The decision barred the dumping of mine tailings into the Yuba River, effectively ending large-scale hydraulic mining. The decision has the distinction of probably being the first court decision in the United States intended to affect the environment in a positive manner.

Hydraulic mining near French Corral, north of Nevada City, before the practice was halted by the Sawyer Decision in 1884.

The Chinese

At the beginning of 1849 there were reportedly 54 Chinese in California. With news of the gold strike, a steady Chinese immigration began; by 1852 there were 15,000 to 20,000 Chinese in California. Contributing to this influx was the poverty and ruin in southeastern China resulting from the Taiping rebellion.

Ship owners distributed flyers in all the Chinese ports, touting the riches to be had in California. As the gold fever spread, the ship owners made large sums of money from passage fees. Most Chinese laborers arrived in California indentured, at the very least to the extent of their passage fees.

The Chinese, almost all male, initially engaged in placer mining, often mining only those claims abandoned by, and with the tacit permission of, the previous claim owners. As the placer claims gave out, some Chinese looked for other work, proving invaluable as laborers, cooks, laundrymen and agricultural workers. They were industrious and worked cheaply, often performing tasks no one else would do.

Early Chinese miners lived together in settlements consisting of groups of tents or brush houses, located near their claims, usually along streams or creeks. These settlements were moved frequently as claims played out and new ones were located.

In the first months surface mining in and around Nevada City yielded sufficient gold to enrich all who came. However, as the argonauts continued to pour into the goldfields, the surface claims yielded less and less gold. Foreign miners were resented and white American-born miners, spurred by greed and the U.S. policy of "manifest destiny, accused foreigners of "stealing" gold belonging to them.

White miners hired Chinese laborers to work this 1852 placer operation near Auburn.

In the 1860s and 1870s Chinese laborers moved unbelievable amounts of earth and rock with carts and wheelbarrows to construct beds and lay tracks for the Central Pacific and the Nevada County Narrow Gauge railroads.

As early as 1850 this collective attitude resulted in the passage of the first of several "foreign miner's taxes," intended to discourage mining by non-citizens by heavily taxing their labors, irrespective of their take. French, Mexican and South American miners were soon driven out, leaving most resentment directed toward the Chinese.

The Chinese were the most "different" of all the foreigners because their appearance and culture did not lend itself to assimilation. Like most miners, the Chinese came to America to make money and return home—most had no intention of remaining here. Chinese males who died could not, by custom, be permanently interred here. There would be no family present to carry out the traditional and perpetual obligations required to ensure the deceased's connection to the spirit world. Because burial at home was thought necessary, remains were disinterred within seven to ten years and returned to China. Female remains, however, were not always so accommodated.

Deceased Chinese were buried temporarily in three locations on the outskirts of Nevada City: in the Chinese cemetery near Railroad Avenue, or in a section of the Pine Grove cemetery on Red Dog Road, or on the grounds of the old county hospital on Willow Valley Road. No remains are thought to be interred now at the Chinese cemetery. There are probably some Chinese buried at the hospital cemetery, and there may be some at the Pine Grove cemetery.

Another class of Chinese immigrated to the gold country about 1860. These were merchants who came to Nevada City for the express purpose of opening shops. They rented buildings on upper Commercial Street and opened laundries, restaurants, grocery stores, brothels and opium dens.

An earlier city ordinance adopted in 1858 prohibiting Chinese from residing or doing business within city limits was not enforced. A second exclusionary ordinance adopted in 1879 was rendered moot when a fire swept through the Chinatown district in 1880, displacing all who lived or did business there. A series of discriminatory city ordinances adopted between 1880 and 1882, prohibited brothels on Pine, Commercial and Broad streets and prohibited the transportation of containers on poles carried across the shoulders.

Similarly, a new fire ordinance was designed to thwart Chinese efforts to rebuild after the fire. Discouraged from remaining in the city, the Chinese relocated to a ravine area outside the city that soon became known as "Kentsville" because Charles Kent, the owner, had invited them to occupy it.

There were few Chinese women in Nevada City—only 40 as counted by the 1860 census and 27 as counted by the 1870 census. Those who entered the United States came as "wives" or "daughters" and had immigrated before Congress passed the Naturalization Act in 1870. This act excluded Chinese from citizenship, and the wives of Chinese laborers were denied entry into the United States. This law was continued via various extension acts until repealed by the Magnuson Act passed by Congress in 1943.

Until construction of the Central Pacific Railroad reached the Auburn area in 1863 there were sufficient numbers of Mexican and Irish laborers to keep the project on track. However, as construction moved forward, the number of these laborers proved insufficient. The railroad ran a newspaper advertisement in the *Sacramento Union* requesting laborers for the project. To the company's discomfiture, many Chinese responded and at first they were not accepted.

Eventually, out of sheer desperation, the contractor experimented with hiring a few Chinese, and when they proved to be excellent workers (willing to work for lower wages and furnish their own food and chefs) he employed from 10,000 to 12,000 Chinese. The Chinese were non-confrontational, were seldom sick, and, when work was scarce they would return to China if they could afford to.

Six years after the transcontinental railroad was finished in 1869, about 300 Chinese were hired to work on the Nevada County Narrow Gauge Railroad because of their proven skills at grading, filling and blasting roadways. Although they were an integral part of the construction of the Central Pacific and the Nevada County Narrow Gauge railroads, the Chinese were excluded from the opening ceremonies of both.

Prior to the relocation to Kentsville, the hub of Chinese commerce and social activity in Nevada City was the intersection of Commercial and York Streets. The Chinese temple of worship, called a Joss, was located on upper Commercial Street, as were general stores, gambling halls, opium dens and theaters. The Chinese gradually moved from the county as gold mining became less productive. All that remains of the Chinese quarter in Nevada City are six buildings once owned or rented by Chinese that are currently the object of a revitalization effort. New Chinatown, or Kentsville, disappeared in the 1920s, and the site is covered by the Golden Center Freeway.

This building on Commercial Street once housed the Sin Lee Laundry before it became an art studio and gallery in the 1960s.

Transportation

Mules, Boats and Stagecoaches

Mules brought the early miners and supplies to the gold camps. As trails improved, mountain wagons or prairie schooners drawn by mules, horses or oxen supplanted pack mules. As the first gold strikes tended to be near rivers or streams, supplies thereafter came by boat, primarily by way of the Sacramento and San Joaquin Rivers and to a lesser extent the American and Yuba Rivers.

As later gold strikes were often not discovered near water, roads became necessary to get supplies to the mines and miners. Roads widened from trails brought the stagecoaches, first to the San Francisco and San Jose areas, then to Sacramento and Marysville and thereafter to the mining camps and communities.

Eastern-transplant Jim Birch's stage company was probably the first to extend service from Sacramento to the mother lode and northern mines in 1851. Birch was able to extend his service in part because of his use of Concord coaches—built in New Hampshire since 1813 and considered the finest coach made. Its distinguishing feature, apart from its overall craftsmanship, was thoroughbracing: two heavy leather straps from which the coach was suspended and which extended to the team's harnesses. Although thoroughbracing provided a vast improvement in passenger comfort, its primary purpose was to provide shock absorbency for the team as it traveled over ruts and other road obstructions. Thoroughbracing allowed teams of horses to travel faster and farther without putting their health at risk.

As the stagecoach business became more competitive, Birch negotiated the merger of competing stagecoach companies into

one organization, the California Stage Company, which then served most mining communities. The smallest mining communities were usually served by one or more express companies, one of which was operated by Nevada City businessman Hamlet Davis, whose company had a customer base of 1500 people.

By 1880 there was a stage line from Nevada City to Marysville via Grass Valley, Rough and Ready, Timbuctoo and Smartsville and a line from North San Juan to Marysville via Sweetland, Birchville, French Corral and Mooney Flat. A third line ran twice daily between Nevada City and Grass Valley. Stagecoach service steadily declined with the advent of the railroad.

Central Pacific Railroad

After completing a project for the Sacramento Valley Railroad, civil engineer Theodore Judah came to Nevada City in October 1860, hoping to discover a practical railroad route over the Sierra.

Judah was aware of Congress's intent to construct a transcontinental railroad system as such discussions had been going on since the early 1850s, although without significant progress. What had been decided, however, was that the railroad would start at two points: one in the Midwest heading west, the other starting in San Francisco or Sacramento heading east, the two to meet in Utah.

In Nevada City Judah met with surveyor Charles Marsh. The pair surveyed several possible routes, ultimately agreeing on a route over Donner Pass, a route that would pass through Colfax. Judah, Marsh and Dutch Flat resident Daniel Strong thereafter agreed to solicit subscriptions for their new undertaking, the Central Pacific Railroad.

Fortuitously, Judah met Sacramento merchant Collis Huntington and thereafter Huntington's business associates including Leland Stanford, Charles Crocker and Mark Hopkins, all of whom agreed to support the railroad venture. The Central Pacific Railroad was incorporated on April 30, 1861. The first board of directors included Judah, Marsh, Strong, Stanford, Huntington, Crocker and Hopkins.

After a two-year wait for congressional backing and the necessary rights-of-way, construction began in Sacramento in January 1863. On May 10, 1869 the Central Pacific met the Union Pacific at Promontory, Utah. Charles Marsh and Leland Stanford

25

were the only Central Pacific directors to attend the final spike ceremonies.

In 1885 the Central Pacific, which had acquired the Southern Pacific in 1868, merged with the Southern Pacific, which had constructed a transcontinental railroad to Louisiana. The merger resulted in Southern Pacific dominating railroad traffic in California.

The Nevada County Narrow Gauge Railroad

In the first years of the gold rush, mining and household supplies were brought into the Nevada City and Grass Valley areas by mule trains from Sacramento. Gold taken from the area by the same mule trains was destined for San Francisco banks. As the communities grew and as placer mining gave way to quartz and hydraulic mining which required heavy machinery, the mule trains and horse-drawn wagons were inadequate because of their inability to carry great weight and because the roads were often impassable during the winter months. Additionally, the emerging orchard and lumber industries required a more efficient, economical and timely transportation method to get their products to the Central Pacific connection in Colfax.

Although there had been many previous attempts to establish a transportation connection between Nevada City and Grass Valley and Colfax, it wasn't until January 24, 1874, that a 20-member committee was formed to finally accomplish such purpose. Ten members from Grass Valley and ten from Nevada City made up the committee.

The Nevada City members included Nat P. Brown, owner and editor of the *Nevada Daily Transcript*; James H. Helm, superintendent of the Pennsylvania Mine; Robert M. Hunt, physician and head of the county hospital; George F. Jacobs, superintendent of the Quaker Hill Mine; Martin Luther Marsh, lumber dealer and county supervisor; Thaddeus Sigourney, director of Citizens Bank; George Smith, county sheriff; Richard W. Tully, owner of the Union Hotel; Niles Searls, attorney and former district judge; and Charles Marsh of the South Yuba Canal Company.

John Coleman of Grass Valley, treasurer of the Idaho Quartz Mining Company, was elected chairman of the group. A steam-powered three-foot narrow gauge railroad was determined to be the most practical choice and was to be constructed without any public funding. A bill was drafted to that effect and was passed by the state legislature on March 20, 1874. The committee began soliciting stock subscriptions and was assured by Leland Stanford that rights-of-way over Central Pacific lands would be granted. Rights-of-way over public lands were secured with the aid of Senator Aaron A. Sargent, a Nevada City resident who carried the enabling bill, subsequently passed by both houses of Congress.

A NCNGRR train made up of freight and passenger cars is pulled by Engine No. 1, an early wood-burning locomotive.

With surveys completed, certificates obtained and sufficient monies obtained, construction of the Nevada County Narrow Gauge Railroad (NCNGRR) was started at Colfax on February 12, 1875. The project, in addition to the rail beds, required construction of two tunnels, five trestles, and bridges over Greenhorn Creek and the Bear River. With construction underway, rolling stock was ordered: two engines (at a cost of $10,000 each), two combination baggage/smoking cars, two passenger cars, seven flatcars and fifteen boxcars.

The project was completed to the Bennett Street terminal in Grass Valley by mid-April 1876 and to Nevada City's Railroad Avenue terminal about one month later. The first regular train service between Nevada City and Colfax was on May 24, 1876. The passenger trains made two daily round trips between Grass Valley/Nevada City and Colfax, and were timed to coincide with the Central Pacific schedules. Round trip tickets between Grass Valley and Colfax cost two dollars, plus an extra dollar to Nevada City.

The first engines used wood as fuel, necessitating several stops to take on wood and water; a one-way trip took about two hours. Later engines used coal, and then oil, which required no stops, thus shortening the trip time.

Freight was shipped by flatcar or boxcar. Although large quantities of various fruit crops and feed for beef and dairy cattle were shipped by railway, lumber shipments accounted for almost one-half of the railroad's freight revenue. During the life of the NCNGRR, gold shipments with an estimated value of $250,000,000 were sent to Colfax in safes installed in the baggage compartment of each combination car. The gold was shipped in ingot form, so heavy that theft would have been difficult. Nonetheless, no extra guards traveled with the gold and there were no robberies of the NCNGRR during its existence.

Of particular interest to locals was the Storms Ranch picnic grounds located about eight miles south of Grass Valley, near what would become Chicago Park. The picnic grounds, which included tables and benches, two bandstands, two dance floors and refreshment booths, were developed in 1877 by John Kidder, then superintendent of the railroad.

Outings to the picnic grounds were by train with special excursion cars, flat cars with bench seating and a canvas top. Trains

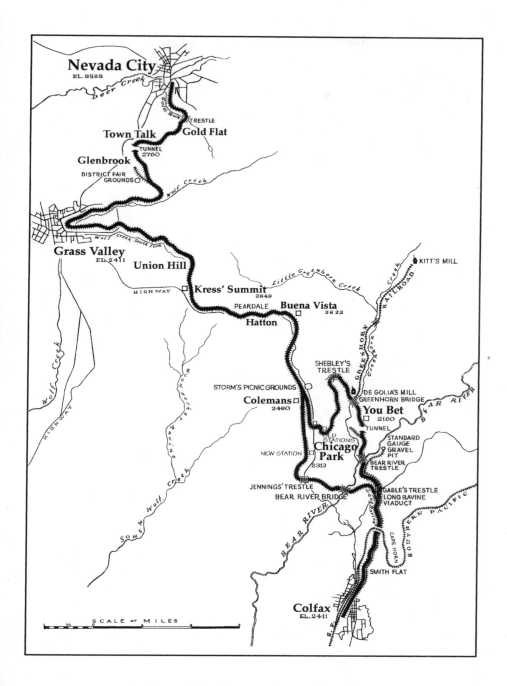

Map of the Narrow Gauge route

**Cloth covers protected picnickers from hot rays of the summer sun
while enroute to Storms Ranch on narrow gauge flatcars.**

to various events at Storms Ranch often pulled 12 excursion cars,
each carrying up to 70 passengers. There were also smaller picnic
grounds, located at Shebley's Grove, also reached by train, and
occasional moonlight excursions to Colfax.

John Kidder, then the majority stockholder of the NCNGRR,
took over the presidency from John Coleman in April 1884. He
remained president until his death in April 1901; his widow, Sara
Kidder, was elected president, a position she held until selling
her stock in 1913. Then the only female railroad president in the
United States, her tenure was marked by many accomplishments
including paying off debt, declaring dividends and generally improving the railroad.

Sam Naphtaly and Walter Arnstein, officers of the Oakland,
Antioch and Eastern Railroad purchased the NCNGRR, immediately transferring the main offices to San Francisco. They kept
the railroad running and made a few improvements, but freight
revenues dissipated in the years after the first world war. As new
highways were being built, the increased use of automobiles and
trucks further cut into the passenger and freight business. The
Sierra Transit Company, a bus line, began service between
Nevada City and Auburn in 1925, further cutting into passenger
revenues.

The NCNGRR requested permission from the Interstate
Commerce Commission to abandon service but, ultimately, the

railroad was transferred back to six Nevada County business-men in exchange for the assumption of the railroad's existing and future indebtedness. The NCNGRR was reorganized and re-capitalized and thereafter showed evidence of prosperity, even through the 1929 stock market crash and subsequent depression, because many gold mines reopened and expanded operations during the 1930s.

In 1935 the NCNGRR entered the trucking business as The Nevada County Trucking Company. In that same year, it began service between Nevada City and Sacramento as the Nevada Pacific Trucking Agency, by agreement with a subsidiary of the Southern Pacific Railroad.

In 1938 the NCNGRR was granted permission by the Inter-state Commerce Commission to abandon passenger service, as the company's busses were already handling most of the pas-senger business; schedules were discontinued in April 1938. The NCNGRR continued operating until March 1942, when it became too valuable as scrap metal for the war effort to continue as a railroad. The last train ran in July 1942.

The NCNGRR was sold to Dulien Steel Products Company of Los Angeles. Some rolling stock was shipped to Alaska and some to Hawaii for military use. Engine No. 5 was purchased by Review Studios (subsequently Universal Studios) where it was used in the 1942 film "The Spoilers," and then retired to a back lot. In 1960 the engine was again revived and used for a variety of television shows including "The Virginians" in 1964 and "Alias Smith and Jones."

Again retired, the engine was brought back to the county in 1985 on a museum loan through the efforts of members of the Transportation Museum Division of the Nevada County Histori-

The original Nevada City train station that served as a model for the Nevada County Historical Society's railroad museum on Kidder Court in Nevada City.

cal Society. In the year 2002 Engine No. 5 became the centerpiece of a new railroad and transportation museum built and owned by the city and operated by the county historical society. The museum, located on Kidder Court (at the juncture of Bost Avenue and New Mohawk Road) and designed to resemble the original Nevada City railroad station, features exhibits of narrow-gauge railroad equipment and rolling stock in various stages of restoration.

Nevada County Traction Company

Although the NCNGRR ran regularly between Nevada City and Grass Valley, it did not go to the town centers. The stagecoach line between the two communities ran every 1½ hours and did a

Happy crowds welcomed Engine No. 5 home in 1985.

brisk business, but the four-mile distance between the towns seemed a "good fit" for an electric trolley. Trolleys in 1901 were already providing service to other parts of California and a line was under consideration to connect Sacramento and Marysville.

The first franchise for a trolley between Nevada City and Grass Valley was granted in 1887 but no progress was made and the franchise lapsed. Many other franchises were granted for the same purpose between 1887 and 1899 but nothing came of any of them. In 1899 John Martin and Eugene de Sabla, area pioneers in supplying hydroelectric power, applied for a franchise to build a five-mile electric railroad between Nevada City and Grass Valley as the first step in an electric railway between Nevada City and Marysville.

Ground was broken in June 1901. The line ran from "Boston Ravine" (near the North Star Power House mining museum in Grass Valley) to Nevada City via East Main Street to Glenbrook, and from there to "Town Talk" (where Banner-Lava Cap Road meets the Nevada City Highway) and followed Searls Avenue and Sacramento Street to Broad Street, crossed the bridge and ended its run at the corner of Pine Street.

Four cars for the line were built in San Francisco, each carrying 44 passengers. Power was provided by two 200-hp generators installed at Glenbrook. Hourly service began October 15, 1901 and continued until 1924, although revenues began to decline about 1912 due to the popularity of the automobile. Fares remained at five cents throughout the life of the trolley, which was permitted to abandon service in January 1925.

A Traction Company street car in front of the National Hotel.

Industry and Commerce

B y the late 1850s weather-related vagaries and waning returns from placer mining were beginning to have an impact on Nevada City. Further, the city's population was depleted by rushes to the Fraser River strike in November 1858 and to the Comstock strike in June 1859.

In 1857 Nevada City merchants went heavily in debt to replace stock lost in the devastating fire of July 19, 1856. Unusually heavy rains during the winter of 1856-1857 made delivery of replacement goods almost impossible. The Laird dam-break in February 1857 resulted in the loss of three businesses and destruction of the Main Street and Broad Street bridges, exacerbating delivery problems.

Logging, Sawmills, Planing Mills

Nevada City was not without an economic base, however. The logging industry was thriving. The primary markets for timber were the quartz mines, which required lumber for shaft bracing, tunnel construction, tunnels, dams and flumes, and the railroads, particularly the Central Pacific, which required lumber for track ties and snow sheds.

Eventually, even as the mines required less support timber and initial Central Pacific Railroad construction was completed, new markets were created for milled Sierra lumber, shipped by rail to Utah's Great Basin for building construction, and to Southern California to make boxes to ship fruit.

The first sawmill was constructed in Nevada City in 1850 by Joshua N. "Nick" Turner, remembered in part for building the Nevada Hotel from the lumber of a single tree. By 1858 there were 42 sawmills in Nevada County, 26 powered by steam, 16 by waterwheels.

First built on Washington Street (behind the courthouse, the Hughes steam-planing mill was relocated to a building at the south end of the Pine Street Bridge after the original mill was destroyed in the November 8, 1863, fire. The plant manufactured doors, sash, blinds and moldings.

Nevada City's most prominent lumberman was Martin Luther Marsh who acquired his first sawmill and timber acreage in the late 1850s, eventually owning several mills as well as an interest in a Nevada City sash factory. Marsh's family home on Boulder Street still stands and is registered as an historic landmark.

Foundries

Edward Coker started the Nevada Iron Foundry and Machine Shop in 1855 on Spring Street behind the National Hotel. After the foundry was destroyed in the July 19, 1856 fire, Coker sold the machinery to David Thom, Thomas J. Williams and J. Jones, who began business on Spring Street near Bennett Street, then built a facility on the foundry's present site at Spring and Bridge streets.

Through several ownership and name changes, the foundry operated blacksmith, machine and pattern shops, and manufactured equipment—stamp mills, water wheels and tools—for the mining industry. In 1957 it became a steel fabrication facility, operating as such until 1974, when it reopened as a Victorian museum and community center devoted to cultural activities. Today it is known as the Miners Foundry.

Breweries

By 1858 there were five breweries in Nevada City. The oldest was probably that of Emile Weiss, a French-born, German-trained brewer who, after walking from Sacramento to Nevada City, established his Nevada Brewery in August 1850. It was destroyed in the 1856 fire but Weiss rebuilt it, along with a residence and barns, on four acres of land.

Louis Dreyfus, after a six-year career as a baker in Nevada City, in 1861 established the Milwaukee Brewery on Spring Street. Dreyfus was city treasurer from 1878–1880 and was the last person buried in the Nevada City Jewish Cemetery (1890).

John Blasauf, born in Switzerland, owned the City Brewery on Pine Street in 1855. After it burned in the 1856 fire he removed his business to Spring Street, and in the summer of 1860 he also had a saloon in Red Dog. His wife Mary owned the brewery in 1880. Louis Siebert established a brewery on Piety Hill in 1878, making cronk beer (non-alcoholic), as well as wine and brandy.

John Blasauf's City Brewery (left) was on South Pine Street in 1856; from 1893 to 1911 Simon Hieronimus manufactered beer in the old stone brewery on Sacramento Street (right).

Casper Fogeli was also a Nevada City brewer but little is known of him or his brewery. Simon Hieronimus came to America from France in 1872, and worked as a brewer at Nevada City from 1876 to 1878. After making beer at North Bloomfield for two years he returned to Nevada City and built a brewery on what is now Searls Avenue. The building burned in 1893 and from then until he died in 1911 he produced his product in the stone building on Sacramento Street.

Flouring Mills

Three flouring mills flourished in Nevada City in the mid-1880s. The Nevada City Flouring Mill was built on Gold Run in 1856, the Buffalo Mill was erected just south of Nevada City in 1857 and Oliver M. Tomlinson built the Elevator Flouring Mill on Manzanita Hill in 1860.

Other Industry

Other light industry in Nevada City during the early to mid 1860s included the Nevada Tannery, built near the county hospital in 1863 and the Pacific Soap Works, a short-lived business started on Coyote Street in 1866 by J. B. Henry, who later (1873) owned a lodging house on Bridge Street.

Nevada City was also distribution center for produce grown in the Peardale and Chicago Park regions of the county and for livestock raised in the Penn Valley area. A trade relationship was established with the Nevada communities of Carson City and Virginia City, towns otherwise unable to sustain themselves.

Commerce in Nevada City circa 1880

6 hotels	3 livery stables	6 wagon/blacksmith shops
4 breweries	3 saloons	1 pipe manufacturer
4 meat markets	9 grocery stores	1 sash and door factory
1 foundry	4 drug stores	1 boot and shoe store
1 bank	1 post office	2 furniture stores
2 lumber yards	2 newspapers	2 book and stationary stores
4 variety stores	1 gas works	1 hardware store
3 tobacco shops	1 crockery store	1 Wells Fargo Express office
3 jewelry stores	5 restaurants	1 photography gallery
6 physicians	2 dentists	1 harness and saddlery shop
11 lawyers	1 theater	

The Nevada City foundry operated under various names over the years. Today it houses a cultural center and is known as the Miners Foundry.

William Holmes was the proprietor of this harness and saddlery business in the nineteenth century.

Blacksmith William Barton operated a shop on Coyote Street (near the corner of Church Street) from the 1850s until his retirement.

Early Nevada City Newspapers

The population of Nevada City in 1850 was 2683; in 1860 the city boasted 3679 citizens and in ten years later 3960 souls were in residence. It is most remarkable that a community of that size was able to support not just one, but three newspapers published simultaneously between 1853 and 1863, and two others published simultaneously between 1864 and 1874.

Nevada Journal

On April 19, 1851, Warren B. Ewer published the first edition of Nevada County's first newspaper, the *Nevada Journal*. It was the second newspaper published in the mines, the first being the *Sonora Herald* which premiered in July 1850. Earlier papers in northern California were the *Sacramento Union* (March 1851), the *San Francisco Herald* (June 1850) and the *Alta California* (January 1849). The *Journal* was published twice weekly through April 1852, weekly until February 1862 and thrice weekly until its demise in November 1863. The paper operated from offices at various Broad Street locations until February 1854, and thereafter at several Main Street locations until November 1863.

Politics

The *Journal* began as a politically neutral newspaper and remained so through a succession of publishers and editors until July 1852, when ownership passed to Aaron Sargent and Edwin R. Budd. From that time until July 1855, again through a succession of publishers and editors, the paper adopted the Whig platform. The American Whig Party was formed in 1834 by a loose coalition of political groups who, desirous of a national economic policy as championed by their antecedent group, the National Republicans, opposed the perceived executive tyranny of Andrew Jackson and his followers.

In July 1855 John P. Skelton, Nat P. Brown and Edwin Waite assumed ownership, with Waite serving as editor. The paper at this time adopted the politics of the American Party, also called the "Know Nothing Party," founded in New York City in 1849. The party's platform was based on native Protestants' resentment of the influx of Roman Catholic immigrants from Europe, primarily Ireland, and their subsequent political impact in large cities.

In 1858, in addition to the American Party platform, the *Journal* adopted the stance of a Stephen Douglas Democrat, a position taken by the northern faction of the Democratic Party that opposed slavery. In the interim, the *Journal*'s Main Street office was destroyed in the fire of July 19, 1856. The office was immediately rebuilt and, being then a weekly, missed only two issues.

In 1861 the paper adopted the Republican Party platform (Lincoln, a Republican, had recently been elected President over a Democratic Party divided over the issue of slavery) and remained so until November 8, 1863, when a city fire destroyed the plant and production ceased.

Owners and Editors

Warren Ewer had worked at the San Francisco *Pacific News* and the Sacramento *Placer Times* before founding the *Journal* in 1851. He sold it a few months later and in 1853 he managed the *Young America* at Nevada City. He was associated with the Grass Valley *Telegraph* and the *Grass Valley National* from 1854 to 1863 and founded the *California Mining Journal* in 1856. From 1862 to 1895 he was editor and part owner of the *Mining and Scientific Press* in San Francisco.

William G. Alban, a subsequent owner with Aaron A. Sargent in 1851–1852, was a Nevada City physician and pharmacist. Sargent, who sporadically edited the *Journal* between 1851 and 1856, was elected district attorney for a term in 1855 and subsequently served in the House of Representatives and the U.S. Senate.

Edwin G. Waite, a co-owner and editor of the paper off and on between 1855 and 1861, left the *Journal* abruptly in 1861 to edit the rival *Morning Transcript*, until 1864. He served in the state assembly in 1855 and in the state senate in 1856–57. Waite was elected Nevada County Treasurer in 1861 and served as political reporter for the San Francisco *Times* and the Sacramento *Union*, was appointed U.S. Naval Officer of San Francisco in 1873, and elected California Secretary of State in 1890.

Nathaniel P. Brown, copublisher of the paper from 1855–1859, was thereafter publisher or copublisher and sporadic editor of the *Morning Transcript* (later called the *Nevada Daily Transcript*) from 1860 to 1903.

Benjamin B. Brierly, briefly editor of the *Journal* from March 1862 until his death in July 1863, was also pastor of the Nevada City Baptist Church. Addison Niles edited the paper for several months in 1855–1856 and again in early 1857 during Edwin Waite's absences to serve in the legislature. Thereafter he was the county judge from 1863 to 1870, and a member of California's supreme court from 1872 to 1879.

Young America / Nevada Democrat

First published on September 14, 1853 by William M. Stewart and Robert A. Davidge, *Young America* was Nevada City's second newspaper, a rival to the *Nevada Journal*. *Young America* was published weekly from its inception (in 1854 the name was changed to *Nevada Democrat*) until September 1860. It was thereafter published thrice weekly from several Broad Street office locations until publication ceased on May 9, 1863. Like most other buildings in Nevada City, the *Nevada Democrat* office was destroyed in the fire of July 19, 1856 fire. The building was quickly rebuilt with the loss of only four weekly issues.

Politics

Young America embraced principles of the Democratic Party. On February 1, 1854 the paper changed its name to the *Nevada Democrat*. When the party split over the slavery issue in 1858, the paper opted for the Stephen Douglas-Democrat position that opposed slavery.

The office of the *Nevada Democrat* (left) was destroyed when Davis's brick block was gutted by fire in 1856. In 1880 the *Tri-Weekly Herald* (right) occupied the upper floor of a brick building built in 1853 at Pine and Broad streets that still stands.

Until the *Transcript* went out of business in 1903, its Commercial Street offices were in the building in the center of this 1960s photo.

Owners and Editors

Young America's first publisher was William Morris Stewart, who functioned in that capacity until June 1854. He was appointed district attorney in 1853, held a temporary post as attorney general of California in 1854-55, and subsequently served several terms in the U.S. Senate representing the state of Nevada.

Tallman Rolfe, who held office as publisher, printer and/or editor of the *Young America/Nevada Democrat* between December 1853 and June 1854, and from January 1857 until the paper's closing, was elected justice of the peace for Nevada Township in 1853. He served on the county board of supervisors from 1859 to 1862 and owned the *Nevada Daily Gazette* from 1863 to 1865. Prior to coming to Nevada City he had worked for the *Oregon Spectator* (1846–47), the *California Star* at San Francisco Bay (1847–48), the *Index* and the *Placer Times* at Sacramento (1850–1851). In 1850 he was a justice of the peace at Yuba City and an associate justice of the Sutter County court of sessions.

His brother Ianthus Rolfe, who was owner or co-owner of the *Democrat* from February 1854 until the paper ceased publication in May 1863.

Warren B. Ewer (see *Nevada Journal* above) managed *Young America* from its inception in 1853 through February 1854.

The Morning Transcript / Nevada Daily Transcript / Miner Transcript

Published by Nat P. Brown, James Allen, John P. Skelton and Andrew Casamayou, *The Morning Transcript* was Nevada City's first daily paper; its first issue was distributed on September 6, 1860. Owned or co-owned by Nat Brown from its inception until 1903, the paper was variously edited during its forty-year existence by

Brown, James Allen, Edwin Waite, Oliver P. Stidger, B. J. Watson, Leonard S. Calkins and Marcellus S. Deal.

Politics

For the bulk of its existence, the *Transcript* was Republican.

Owners and Editors

In addition to his newspaper duties, Nat P. Brown, with John K. Dallison, published the *Nevada Directory* in 1856. Brown was a member of the board of town trustees in 1877.

Oliver P. Stidger, who edited the *Nevada Daily Transcript* in 1873, was part owner of the *Hydraulic Press* (1861), the *San Juan Press* (1863–1864), and edited the *San Juan Times* (1874–78). He owned the San Juan Theater in 1874 and was a superintendent of the San Juan Irrigating Company. Before coming to Nevada County Stidger served as justice of the peace at Foster's Bar and was an associate justice on the Yuba County court of sessions. In 1853–1854 he had been part owner and editor of the *Marysville Herald.*

B. J. Watson, elected county superintendent of schools in 1872, became co-owner and editor of the *Daily Transcript* in 1873, founded the *Nevada Weekly Gazette* in 1876, and was elected state senator from Nevada and Sierra Counties in 1879. He bought the *Truckee Republican* newspaper in 1880, and was appointed Port Warden at San Francisco in 1891.

Leonard S. Calkins was born at Selby Flat near Nevada City in 1853 but grew up in Ohio, Illinois, and Kansas. He returned to Nevada City in 1877 and worked for the the *Nevada Transcript* for a year before becoming part owner and editor in October 1878. He founded the *Colfax Sentinel* in 1890 and retired from both papers in February 1892 when he was appointed postmaster at Nevada City. In 1903 he began editing *The Daily Miner* for the Calkins Newspaper Syndicate, which bought the *Daily Transcript* in 1904 and merged it with the *Miner*. The *Miner–Transcript*, ceased publication on December 31, 1907.

Nevada Daily Gazette

First published on March 9, 1864 by Oliver Stidger (later associated with the *Nevada Daily Transcript*) and Ianthus Rolfe (co-publisher of the *Nevada Democrat* 1854–1863), the *Nevada Daily Gazette* was published daily with a Monday weekly in December 1867.

Politics

Politically, the paper was pro-Union (Republican).

Owners and Editors

Edwin F. Bean, the first Republican postmaster at Nevada City (1861–65) became owner and editor of the paper in November 1866 and either owned or co-owned the *Gazette* until publication ceased in 1874. He is probably best known for publishing *Bean's Directory of Nevada County*. In 1872–73 he was co-owner of the Virginia City *Evening Chronicle*.

Tri-Weekly Herald

Devoted primarily to mining issues, the *Tri-Weekly Herald* was founded and published by J. B. Gray, E. A. Davis and Henry L. Herzinger. The paper first appeared in 1878 and is known to have continued publication until at least 1900, when Frank Wadsworth acquired ownership.

Politics

The political leaning of the paper, if any, is unknown.

Owners and Editors

J. B. Gray was elected town marshal in 1874 but little else is known with respect to the paper's principals.

Before the introduction of typesetting machines, all Nevada County news stories were set by hand, one letter at a time.

Fires and Fire Companies

By April 1850, with its assortment of tents, shanties and board houses, the newly named Nevada City began to take on the appearance of a town. Shortly, several hotels, saloons and stores sprang up on Broad, Main and Commercial Streets. In July 1850 the town limits were extended to accommodate new growth.

Merchants stored large quantities of merchandise in anticipation of a severe winter but little rain fell during the winter of 1850–1851 and there was, as a consequence, no water to work the mines. The price of goods plummeted, merchants failed and Nevada City's prosperity appeared to be coming to an end. Contrary to the dire predictions, however, 1851 began actively, with at least 250 buildings in town and many more tents and cabins in the surrounding area. Businesses rebounded and mining activity was on the increase.

Then, on March 11, 1851, a fire, thought to have been deliberately set in a saloon at Main and Commercial Streets, destroyed more than 100 buildings and hundreds of thousands of dollars in merchandise. Afterward, thought was given to fire prevention and more substantial building construction, but in the end the town was rebuilt with inexpensive clapboard structures.

Eighteen months later, on September 7, 1852, another fire started east of Deer Creek where Broad, Boulder, Sacramento and Nevada Streets intersect—a business area then (and now) known as the Plaza—destroying 12 businesses. Again there was discussion of fire prevention and this time something was accomplished. A fire patrol was organized, Gold Run creek was tapped and a water pipe installed, terminating at a standpipe at the intersection of Broad and Pine Streets.

Hamlet Davis, who was developing that area of town, spearheaded the water project. He had built a two-story frame building with a market and express office on the first floor and Nevada City's first theater, Dramatic Hall, on the second floor that was also used as a public reading room.

Merchants on Main Street then installed a waterline the length of the street using a pump that drew water from Deer

Creek. Both the Broad Street and Main Street efforts were re-warded when fires on November 28, 1854 (which destroyed nine homes on Main Street), and on February 20, 1855 (which burned 16 homes on Broad Street), did not wipe out the entire city.

Establishment of a city-wide fire department was difficult because merchants on Main Street were engaged in a rivalry, sometimes acrimonious, with merchants on Broad Street as to which street was more important.

In 1853 Broad Street merchant Hamlet Davis constructed a so-called "fireproof" brick building in Nevada City at the corner of Pine and Broad Streets next to his Dramatic Hall. Soon there were 28 brick buildings interspersed with the city's frame struc-tures, and discussions of a fire department waned.

By the summer of 1856 Nevada City was the third largest city in California and, because of its gold production, possibly the most important. Times were good and there had not been a major fire in more than a year.

Disaster struck on July 19, 1856, however, when embers from a forge at William Hughes' blacksmith shop on South Pine Street ignited the bellows, then the adjacent wall. Within minutes the whole town was engulfed; more than 400 buildings including more than 20 of the supposedly fireproof brick buildings were destroyed. More importantly, at least ten people died in the fire, most of whom had remained in the brick buildings, thinking them safe.

One of those killed was Hamlet Davis's nephew, who had stayed behind in his uncle's brick building. Bankrupt and feeling responsible for those who had died in his building, Davis dis-posed of his holdings and moved to Dutch Flat. A month after the fire, however, more than 200 structures had been built and the brick buildings were being repaired.

On May 23, 1858, 200 wood buildings were destroyed by fire but 30 brick structures survived, including the then-new courthouse and the National Exchange Hotel.

Finally, in late 1859, steps were taken toward forming a fire department. Because the merchants of both Broad Street and Main Street wanted the fire department headquarters on their street, two fire companies were formed. On June 12, 1860, the Nevada Hose Company No. 1 was established, headquartered on Main Street. A day later, on June 13, 1860, the Eureka Hose Com-

Main Street's Firehouse No. 1 as it once looked (left) and in its present-day garb as a the county's first historical museum (right).

pany No. 2 was organized, headquartered on Broad Street. A third Company, the Protection Hook and Ladder Company No. 1 was organized November 22, 1860, and was the first to occupy a structure, a wooden building constructed on Broad Street. However, the company quickly disbanded and its volunteer members joined one of the two other companies.

Though second to organize, the Eureka Company, through the fundraising efforts of the city's women, was first to occupy its own building on upper Broad Street, a building which still stands and is one of the most photographed buildings in Nevada City.

The Nevada Hose Company moved into its Main Street quarters on May 30, 1861. The building is presently operated as a public museum by the Nevada County Historical Society.

The Nevada and Eureka Companies soon consolidated, creating the Nevada City Fire Department. The Eureka Hose Company purchased from the Pennsylvania Engine Company No. 12 of San Francisco a beautifully painted and lettered horse-drawn fire wagon. Not wanting to deface the wagon, the Eureka Hose Company changed its name to the Pennsylvania Engine Company No. 2, removing only the "1" from the "12" and re-painting that small area.

On July 7, 1860, engineer Charles Marsh's offer to provide free fire-fighting water to the city in exchange for a 20-year franchise to sell water to the community was accepted. Marsh built a reservoir on Buckeye Hill, behind the present Helling Library at the county government center off Highway 49. Marsh then laid two miles of pipe and installed 28 hydrants throughout the city. Maintenance of the system was contractually to be the responsibility of the town trustees. The project was completed in a matter of months.

Responding to a fire at the Red Rock Saloon on November 8, 1863, firefighters connected to the hydrants. Minutes later the water stopped—the lines, never having been flushed, were clogged and useless. The fire quickly spread and Nevada City was again destroyed.

The fire department thereafter gained control of the water system and Nevada City has not had a city-wide fire since. There have, of course, been significant fires that could have caused widespread losses (such as the Union Hotel conflagration of 1908 and the Elks Club fires of 1914 and 2002), but they were contained by well-trained and well-equipped fire fighters, provided with ample supplies of water.

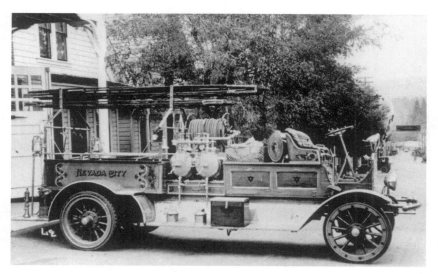

This Seagrave 1913 combination chemical pumper was the first motorized truck in the city's fire department.

Looking north from Deer Creek in 1908 when the Union Hotel lost its roof and third floor to fire. The hotel continued to operate with only two stories until it was removed (along with other historic buildings shown in this photo) to accommodate the freeway.

Firemen fighting the Pine Street blaze that consumed the historic Elks Lodge building on March 20, 2002.

Entertainment

The Early Days

Not unlike their counterparts in other mining communities of the Mother Lode and the Northern Mines, Nevada City miners soon demanded entertainment after their labors—entertainment which would include alcohol, music, dancing, gambling and women.

Not surprisingly, the first "entertainment" was the saloon followed by the gambling hall (usually in conjunction with a saloon). Music, often basic stringed instruments, encouraged dancing; soon, women began their foray into the mining camps.

The finest gambling saloons in Nevada City in 1851 were the Empire, on Main Street, and Barker's Exchange, opposite the Empire, with entrances on both Broad and Main streets. Although constructed of shake and canvas, the interiors of such establishments were relatively opulent. These "gambling hells" employed musicians and provided tables where players enjoyed faro, twenty-one, monte and roulette. Miners also enjoyed and

The Empire gambling saloon on Main Street appears on the right side of this 1852 daguerreotype of Nevada City.

bet on bear and bull fights, staged in arenas set up on Broad Street, and also bet on chicken fights, dogfights and prizefights.

Interest in these entertainments appears to have lessened concurrently with the improvement of roads between Nevada City and Sacramento and San Francisco. Better roads and the Concord stagecoach made travel between the cities quite bearable and brought first-rate entertainers and acting troupes to the goldfields. These performers, from Europe and the East Coast, worked their way west to gold-rich mining communities which included Nevada City, Grass Valley, Red Dog, You Bet, Marysville, Oroville and Dutch Flat by way of San Francisco and Sacramento.

Nevada City residents, many of whom were from large eastern and midwestern cities and were relatively cultured, welcomed more sophisticated entertainment. As Nevada City developed, the miners took wives or sent for their spouses and started families, became involved with churches and fraternal organizations and gradually became acclimated to more acceptable forms of entertainment.

Live Theater

The first theatrical activities in Nevada City were held in a building constructed by Nevada City merchant Hamlet Davis who, during the summer of 1851, modified the public reading room on the second story of his business, located on the northeast corner of Broad and Pine Streets, into a theater. Called Dramatic Hall, the theater opened with the Robinson Troupe, headed by "Yankee" or "Doc" Robinson, a Yale-educated physician. After opening a pharmacy in San Francisco and converting it to accommodate theatrical performances (of which he was the principal attraction), he formed a touring company, which included his wife and son, and toured until his death in 1856.

Dramatic Hall was the only theater in Nevada City until Charles Lovell, owner of the Empire gambling saloon, built the Jenny Lind Theatre at the foot of Main Street, a structure which projected over Deer Creek. The Chapman Family troupe, among the first of the acting companies to arrive in California from the east coast, opened the theater on November 20, 1851, with three farces. The Jenny Lind's existence in Nevada City was short-lived, however, as a major storm flooded Deer Creek in March

1851, dislodging the underpinnings of the structure and carrying it downstream where it disintegrated near the Pine Street bridge.

Dramatic Hall continued as the only theater in Nevada City until Lyman Frisbie, owner of a restaurant and saloon, opened Frisbie's Concert Hall at the intersection of Main and Coyote streets on June 6, 1854. The theater opened with the H. A. Warwick Troupe's production of Shakespeare's *Merchant of Venice.*

The theater was destroyed by fire on July 19, 1856, and Frisbie, with a new partner, architect and builder Charles H. Bain, erected the Nevada Theatre (not to be confused with the later and present Nevada Theatre) on the site of the former concert hall. This theater continued operating until destroyed by fire on May 23, 1858.

Built on Main Street after Frisbie's Nevada Theatre burned, the Metropolitan was opened on September 16, 1858, by the California Minstrels. They had previously introduced the melodeon (an accordion-like instrument) to Nevada City during an 1855 performance at Dramatic Hall. The Metropolitan presented performances until destroyed, along with most of downtown Nevada City, in the fire of November 8, 1863.

One of the two Temperance Halls was built on lower Sacramento Street near the intersection of Boulder Street. The hall was built by John L. Williams, an early pioneer in the effort to bring piped water to Nevada City. The date of its construction is not known, although events were held there as early as 1853 and it burned in the fire of 1856, along with his waterworks.

Williams rebuilt the Temperance Hall after the fire and it was used for a temporary court room in 1857. Even though it wasn't built as a theater, it nonetheless occasionally functioned as such, particularly between 1859 and 1865 when no other theatrical facilities existed in Nevada City. Church services and court proceedings were also held there after destructive fires. Mrs. Blum purchased the hall in 1864 and had it remodeled.

The second Nevada Theatre rose from the ruins of the fire-ravaged Bailey House hotel at Broad and Bridge streets. The first event held there was a memorial service for President Lincoln soon after his assassination in 1865. In September the theater opened officially with the comic drama *The Dutch Governor* and the Worrell Sisters in a burlesque performance of *Cinderella.*

Of the visiting artists to perform in Nevada City during its

Junius Booth Jr. and Edwin T. Booth ca. 1857–1858

theatrical heyday, Edwin Booth would become the country's leading Shakespearean actor. Brother of Lincoln's assassin, John Wilkes Booth, young Edwin traveled with his father and another brother, Junius Booth Sr. and Jr., and acted in his father's productions. Booth performed at Dramatic Hall in October, November and December 1852 and returned to Nevada City for performances in February and August 1856. Even at this early point in his career, Booth's acting talent was recognized by local theatergoers and the media.

Possibly the most notorious performer to appear in Nevada City was Lola Montez, a Grass Valley resident during the years 1853-1855. Montez, described as attractive but an unexceptional dancer and actress, was best known for her off-stage antics and status as an international courtesan, having had liaisons with Franz Liszt, Alexandre Dumas, Honoré de Balzac and Ludwig, King of Bavaria, among others.

Montez gave several performances at Dramatic Hall during the week of July 25–29, 1853. Aaron Sargent, then editor of the *Nevada Journal* and thought to be the most knowledgeable of the local theater reviewers, reported large audiences for Montez' performances at twice the usual ticket prices and noted that she "exhibited herself here in a most gracious mood."

Lotta Crabtree, who would become a much more significant force in theater than Montez, appeared with the Metropolitan Troupe at Frisbie's Nevada Theater on July 1 and 2, 1857. The Metropolitan Troupe was not particularly well received, but Lotta's talent, even as a ten-year-old, was easily recognized. In

August 1858 Lotta again appeared in Nevada City at Temperance Hall for four nights with the John Potter Troupe.

Another notable who appeared locally was Catherine (Kate) Hayes, the Irish-born soprano called "The Swan of Erin" or "The Irish Nightingale" who studied in France and Italy. She toured the United States in 1851 and, after tours in San Francisco and Sacramento, appeared at Dramatic Hall in Nevada City on April 18, 1853. Critics lauded her "beautiful voice" but described her as an "imperfect musician" who didn't work at her craft. Hayes was rumored to have had a romantic affair with notorious area outlaw Rattlesnake Dick in 1853, but the alleged dalliance could not be confirmed.

American-born composer and pianist Louis Moreau Gottschalk, a child prodigy and student of Hector Berlioz in France, became one of the best-known and popular American artists of the mid-nineteenth century. A western United States tour in 1865 included critically acclaimed concerts at Temperance Hall in Nevada City on June 16 and 17, 1865.

Mark Twain appeared twice at the Nevada Theatre in Nevada City, lecturing on the Sandwich (Hawaiian) Islands on October 23, 1866, returning for another lecture in 1868.

The Nevada Theatre before it was a movie house.

The Broadway cinema, across Broad Street from the National Hotel.

World-famous operatic soprano Emma Nevada (nee Emma Wixom) was born in Nevada County and lived a short time in Nevada City where she gave her first public performance at age three. She was thereafter raised in the state of Nevada until returning to California to attend Mills College in Oakland. After a successful opera career in Europe and America, she visited Nevada City during her last American tour, giving a memorable performance to an appreciative, overflow audience at the Nevada Theatre on March 31, 1902.

Movie Theaters

Then just a novelty, Nevada City's first motion picture venue, the Crystal Theater, opened on Commercial Street in March 1908. Usually five or six one-reel titles were shown during an evening. There was, of course, no sound.

The Crystal Theater closed in 1909 and in that same year the Broadway Theater, a converted portion of a livery stable located across Broad Street from the National Hotel, opened. Fares were ten cents for adults and five cents for children.

In April 1915 the old Crystal Theater on Commercial Street was remodeled and reopened as the Gem Photo Theater.

Although remodeled in 1908–1909 to accommodate both

motion pictures and vaudeville acts, the Nevada Theatre was again remodeled in 1915 to show films, and opened as The Cedar Theatre. The films were accompanied by a piano until the advent of "talking pictures." The Cedar showed movies until 1958 when its closing was occasioned by the increasing popularity of television.

A local group, calling itself the Liberal Arts Commission, subsequently purchased and rehabilitated the then-vacant building, reopening in 1965 with a gala production of *Golden Days*. The Nevada Theatre currently functions as a venue for both live theater and the occasional showing of films.

The Nevada Theatre, in its reincarnation as The Cedar, looked like this in December 1949, after it had been remodeled in the latest fashion.

Prostitution

A lmost everyone who participated in the gold rush came to the gold fields for the express purpose of making money, and how money was made, short of serious criminal activity, was irrelevant. While illegal, prostitution was viewed by most as a necessary service in the mining and railroad camps, not known during the gold rush as hotbeds of morality.

Prostitution as well as gambling and other fringe services closely followed the Argonauts into the gold fields. While most women arrived by way of San Francisco and Sacramento, some of the first prostitutes to arrive on the West Coast were Latin, having boarded Argonaut-laden ships that had come around Cape Horn. These women, who were obligated for their passage, boarded at South American and Mexican port stops. Upon arriving in San Francisco, the women were sold by ships' captains to saloon owners who required the women to prostitute themselves to repay their indebtedness.

Also arriving early in 1849, on three ships from Australia, were about 200 women, many of whom were prostitutes. Fifty French prostitutes, considered undesirable, arrived in the fall of 1850 after Louis Napoleon, in an attempt to rid France of its criminal element, conducted national lotteries to raise funds to pay passage for these women to America.

The first prostitutes in Nevada City arrived in the spring of 1850. In California the "best" of these ladies worked in bordellos, where their needs were attended to by the house madam. These establishments catered to the better classes and were expensive. These "houses" were often found in conjunction with gambling saloons. A physician regularly examined women working in these houses and there were no reported cases of either venereal disease or rape occurring therein.

Second-tier prostitutes were the streetwalkers; these women were not as refined, educated or attractive as those who worked in bordellos, but were a considerable step up from the lowest class of prostitute, women who worked in "cribs." Cribs were cubicles, some no larger than four by six feet and generally located on run-down streets or in alleyways. Women who offered their services from these locations were generally either older or less attractive destitute women, or women who had been purchased from their families in China by the Tongs and sent to America to make money for their owners.

Most Chinese prostitutes worked in San Francisco, Sacramento or Marysville, although some worked in the gold camps. Many became opium addicts, and sexually transmitted diseases spread unchecked. Chinese prostitutes in Nevada City were not known to have worked from cribs.

The better-known bordellos in Nevada City included the Pavilion House on Broad Street, operated in 1852 by Elizabeth Carrier; the French Saloon, located on the southwest corner of Pine and Commercial Streets and operated by Elizabeth Applegate; and the White Hall, operated by William H. "Billy" Mayfield on Broad street. During one period the wealthiest madam

Eléanore Dumont came to Nevada City in 1852 and operated a Broad Street gambling saloon known as the Polka House. When she died 25 years later at Bodie she was known as "Madame Moustache," a professional prostitute.

in Nevada City was reputed to be Jennie Anderson, whose house could be found at the intersection of Pine and York Streets.

The most infamous house on Spring Street in the early years was probably that of "Old Harriet," who ran a saloon/brothel with her consort. On two separate occasions, men were found dead, minus their clothes and possessions, after leaving her establishment. In later years, from about 1934 to 1952, four brothels, employing 25 women, operated on lower Spring Street (no longer in existence, the street and buildings having been demolished during construction of the Golden Center Freeway in 1966).

Prostitution was not listed as an occupation in the 1860 census; however, it was estimated that there were nine women so employed in Nevada City at that time. The 1870 census showed 12 white and 25 Chinese prostitutes working in the city

Anti-Prostitution Efforts

The Sabbatarians were unsuccessful in their attempts to close businesses on Sunday in 1851, 1853 and 1854. While these efforts were aimed primarily at gambling, similar efforts were directed at prostitution. By 1855 most businesses were closed on Sundays, the result of a state law prohibiting open gambling; efforts to curtail prostitution, however, were less successful.

In 1880 Nevada City enacted an ordinance prohibiting brothels on Pine, Commercial and Broad Streets. In 1900 Nevada City enacted an ordinance banning all "cathouses" on the north side of Spring Street and on either side of National Alley. In 1914 the State of California enacted the Red Light Abatement Act.

None of the aforementioned efforts were entirely successful. It wasn't until 1952 that Attorney General Edmund G. "Pat" Brown permanently closed Nevada City's brothels.

The Pine Street Bridge

The severe winter of 1861–1862 washed out most of Nevada City's bridges, causing a major disruption of transportation services. The Nevada and Grass Valley Turnpike Company decided to build a long-proposed state-of-the-art suspension bridge over Deer Creek to better connect the Grass Valley road to the Nevada City business district.

Bridge contractor Andrew Hallidie (later of San Francisco cable car fame) completed the bridge in June 1862. With a suspended roadway of 4700 square feet, the Pine Street bridge was then the largest suspension bridge in California.

A few weeks later, on July 10, 1862, the bridge collapsed, sending two teamsters and several of the team of oxen to their deaths and injuring two bridge pedestrians. Suits were brought, but neither the city nor the contractors were found liable.

A view of Andrew Hallidie's suspension bridge over Deer Creek (after it was rebuilt in 1862), looking north to the center of the city. This photo shows the uncovered support towers.

The Pine Street suspension bridge after towers were enclosed to protect them against the weather.

The bridge was immediately rebuilt and remained in service until 1901, when it was deemed unsafe for other than foot traffic. A new two-span steel bridge with a plank deck was constructed in 1904 and renamed the Gault bridge in honor of Nevada City civic leader Alex Gault.

The present bridge, built in 1996, is an all-steel replica of the Gault bridge, which, like its predecessor, had become unsafe.

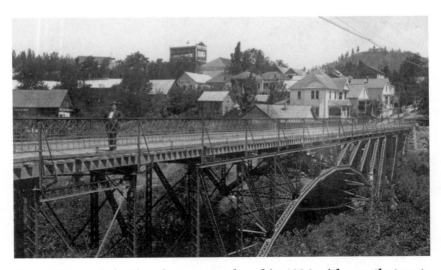

The 1904 Gault bridge that was replaced in 1996 with one that met the state's more stringent safety standards. The tall building on the horizon is the stage end of the Nevada Theatre.

The Freeway, the
Historical Ordinance and the
Downtown Betterment Project

The Golden Center Freeway

By the early 1950s increasing automobile traffic in Nevada City and Grass Valley alerted residents of both communities to the fact that the main road linking the cities, the Nevada City Highway, was or would soon become inadequate.

Although construction would not begin for 15 years, negotiations began between the Nevada City Council and the California State Department of Transportation for the construction of a freeway connecting Nevada City and Grass Valley.

In 1951 a poll of city residents narrowly favored a freeway route that bypassed the city. The alternate route, which bisected part of the city's downtown historical area, was ultimately approved by the City Council, not, however, without polarizing a community whose emotions ran high over the project.

Among the structures to be razed to accommodate freeway construction were the South Yuba River Canal Company (site of the present Chamber of Commerce), the adjacent Ott Assay Office, and the long-vacant Union Hotel. The Canal Company and Ott buildings were saved by a negotiated slight alteration of the freeway route, but all other buildings were razed, as was a giant Sequoia tree that had served for many years as the city's Christmas tree. Also obliterated was lower Spring Street, once Nevada City's red light district.

Right-of-way purchases and budgeting for the nearly three-and-half-mile Nevada City portion of the project, extending from the Glenbrook basin to the eastern edge of Nevada City, was well under way by 1963. That portion of the project was formally dedicated on October 20, 1967.

The Historical Ordinance

Nevada City's many decades of prosperity were due almost sole-

Lower Main Street before the freeway was built. The South Yuba Canal building and Ott's Assay office on the left were preserved, and the Union Hotel (on the right) was torn down.

View from Prospect Hill looking north to Sugar Loaf hill after freeway construction was well underway.

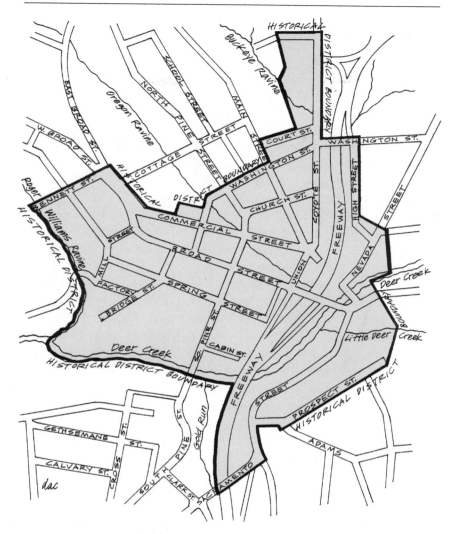

Map of the Nevada City Historical District.

ly to the area's gold mining operations. When the region's last gold mine (the Empire Mine) closed in 1956, Nevada City, with no other viable economic base, found itself in the throes of an economic depression with no apparent resolution.

Many local residents, however, aware of the city's idyllic setting and appreciative of its Mother Lode–type architectural styles, visualized the community as a tourist destination. It was concluded that an ordinance should be drafted to protect the city's heritage. The necessity of such an ordinance was magnified in the mid to late 1960s with the construction of the Golden Center Freeway and the attendant demolition of several historically and architecturally significant buildings.

A precursor to the proposed protection ordinance was an ordinance adopted on March 9, 1964, which essentially outlawed billboards along the proposed freeway route in Nevada City unless specific criteria were met.

Ordinance 338, adopted August 12, 1968, was titled *An Ordinance of the City of Nevada City Establishing an Historical District and Providing Regulations for the Protection, Enhancement and Perpetuation of Buildings Therein*. The ordinance defined the boundaries of the district and provided that the exterior appearance of all buildings within the district constructed or altered after the effective date of the ordinance had to substantially conform to a "Mother Lode" style of architecture.

The characteristics of Mother Lode architecture consisted of wood and brick as primary materials; the design features were gabled or shed roofs, tall and narrow windows and doors, iron or wooden shutters, balconies, wooden awnings and ornamental scrollwork. The ordinance also dealt with the size, style and placement of commercial signs within the Historical District.

The ordinance survives today because it requires "substantial," rather than strict compliance with its provisions, and has been amended only minimally since its adoption, usually with respect to signs or extension of district boundaries.

The Downtown Betterment Project

A federal program—designed to assist communities in becoming more economically viable by improving the physical properties of the business district, and with the stated purpose of creating jobs—provided the impetus for a Nevada City Chamber of Commerce poll of downtown businesses to determine if a physically improved downtown business district would create new jobs.

After receiving positive responses and commitments from businesses, in 1978 the City of Nevada City applied to the Sierra Economic Development District for a $240,000. 80/20 matching funds grant from the federal government

The grant—which was approved—required the repaving of Broad Street from the National Hotel to the Methodist Church and the repaving of Spring Street. The grant also required the construction of two city parking lots—one located behind the National Hotel, the other on Nevada Street, near the freeway overpass. To be renovated were two adjacent buildings on Main Street, which were purchased by the city. The Nevada City Chamber of Commerce presently occupies one of the buildings.

During construction, Pacific Gas and Electric Company removed the overhead power lines in the downtown business district and placed them underground. As part of the federal grant, the streetlights on Broad Street were replaced with gas lamps. Outside the grant, Nevada City replaced the streetlights on Commercial Street with gas lamps.

These improvements, along with the protections afforded by the historical ordinance, have resulted in the present-day downtown business district—not too unlike the Nevada City of the 1860s.

Lower Broad Street at the beginning of the 21st century, gas street lamps and all. The building on the right was built in 1853, and the one in the middle was constructed after the fire of 1856.

Nevada City Today

During the last half of the twentieth century, Nevada City made a remarkable recovery—from a town with no viable economic base and a near lifeless downtown business district—to a thriving community with tourism as its primary economic resource.

Nevada City's near-death experience, beginning in the late 1950s, was attributed by many to the 1957 closing of the Empire Mine, the last operating gold mine in California. While the logging industry provided a living to some, there was, basically, no other industry or commerce.

In the early 1960s some farsighted residents recognized the potential for the city's historical buildings and foothill ambience to attract visitors. The first visible manifestation of this new direction was enactment of the Historical Ordinance in 1968 that protected the city's historical buildings. The ordinance was followed in 1978 by the Downtown Betterment Project, which effected a recapture of some of the flavor of Nevada City's gold rush days.

These community efforts, and the opening of the Golden Center Freeway, which facilitated travel to Nevada City, combined to attract many newcomers to the area, mostly from large urban areas in California. These immigrants—among whom are writers, poets, artists and musicians—collectively contribute to the area's cultural vibrancy and attractiveness as both a tourist destination and as a desirable place to live.

Residents and visitors alike appreciate the annual fall colors, reminiscent of New England, and the classical concerts presented by Music in the Mountains throughout the year. Also enjoyed are the live theater productions of the Nevada Theatre Company, the art galleries, the wine-tasting rooms and the numerous bookshops scattered throughout the business district. Seasonal events, such as Summer Nights in July and Victorian Christmas in December attract many to the downtown streets, as do several parades, including the Fourth-of-July parade, which alternates between Nevada City and Grass Valley, and the Constitution Day parade in September.

Appendix A

Selected Biographies

Daniel S. Baker — Arrived February 11, 1850. Broad Street grocer for 13 years. Ran teaming and freight business until narrow gauge railroad began running in 1876. Trustee of Nevada Theatre Co.

David Belden — Opened law practice in 1855. County judge 1859–1863. State senator 1865–68. Moved to San Jose, where he was a district court judge and superior court judge in Santa Clara Co.

John C. Birdseye — Storekeeper since 1857; private banker 1858–1864, state senator 1863. Purchased flouring mill in 1860. Invested in mine operations.

Nathaniel P. Brown — Part owner of *Nevada Journal* 1855–1859. Founder and publisher of the *Morning Transcript*, first daily newspaper in county, 1860–1904.

John Caldwell — District attorney 1866–1868; state assemblyman 1858–1859; justice of the peace 1869; county judge 1873–1879. Superior court judge 1880–1897.

Thomas H. Caswell — County judge 1851–1859. One of first officers of Trinity Episcopal Church 1855. First man raised into Nevada Lodge #13, F&AM, June 7, 1851.

Nellie Elizabeth Pooler Chapman — At age 14 married dentist Allan Chapman in Nevada City. Practiced dentistry with him, first as assistant then as partner. She was "grandfathered in" when state licensing became mandatory in 1879, and was first woman licensed to practice dentistry in the western United States.

Samuel Clutter — Arrived in 1861. Carriage maker with shops on Broad Street and on the Plaza. Elected to board of town trustees 1872, 1873, and 1874. City treasurer for six terms. Founder of Nevada City Benevolent Society.

Hamlet Davis — Owned first store (a tent) on Broad Street in May 1850. Built two-story frame building corner Broad and Pine streets in 1850. Operated express line, bank and hotel. Erected first brick building in 1853. Was ruined by fire of 1856 and moved to Dutch Flat to raise fruits and vegetables. Opened fruit store in new town of Truckee in 1868 and served as a member of the 1878 California Constitutional Convention.

Warren B. Ewer — First editor-publisher of the *Nevada Journal*, April 1851. He and John Boardman purchased the *Grass Valley Telegraph* in 1854. Owned and sometimes edited the *Telegraph* and the

National until 1863. Founding officer of Nevada City Baptist Church. Moved to San Francisco and edited the *Mining and Scientific Press* 1862–1895.

Lyman P. Frisbie — Built Concert Hall in 1853 next to his wife's saloon and restaurant at Main and Coyote streets. Converted hall to a theater in 1855. After his buildings were destroyed in the fire of 1856 he erected the first Nevada Theatre on the same corner. After the building burned in 1858 Frisbie went to San Francisco to manage the Pacific Museum. In 1860 he and his wife opened a hotel, saloon and restaurant at Carson City, Nevada, which he ran until they burned down in 1878.

Felix Gillet — Operated a barbershop in the 1860s. In early 1870s he imported several varieties of walnuts to Nevada City from France. Introduced filberts, chestnuts and several varieties of grapes to the West Coast.

A. B. Gregory — Crossed plains in 1851 with wife and children to join his parents, siblings and five slaves, all of whom had come to Nevada City in 1850. Grocer and lumberman. Member of school board in 1858, and a town trustee for several terms. Studied law in Nevada City and admitted to bar in 1857.

Thomas Porter Hawley — Deputy county clerk 1855; district attorney 1864–1866. Officer in Nevada Library Association 1858. Moved to state of Nevada in 1868 and was district attorney of White Pine County. Elected to Nevada Supreme Court in 1871 and served as its chief justice 1872–1890. U.S. district court judge 1890–1906.

Moses F. Hoit — Elected mayor of Nevada City in 1851. Part owner of Coyote Water Co. He and William Sublette built toll bridge over South Yuba River at Long Point and a toll road from Nevada City to Columbia Hill and Sweetland. Floodwaters washed the bridge away in December 1861. Rebuilt in 1862, the bridge was owned by Hoit until his death in 1867.

Dr. Robert Menzo Hunt — Mined at Nevada City before joining his brother Harvey's medical practice in 1854. The brothers took charge of the county hospital in 1859. Robert and Harvey performed a successful operation on a patient with an aneurysm in 1861, the first such in Nevada City. Important backer of the narrow gauge railroad, and a founder of the original Citizens Bank.

George Washington Kidd — Arrived with family in 1850. Kept a boarding house, general store. Invested in real estate, mining and water ditches. Opened private bank in 1859. Owner-operator of two steamers on the Sacramento River in the early 1860s.

Dr. William Knox — Came to Nevada City with wife in 1850. Practiced medicine 1851–1861 and invested in real estate and canals. Town trustee 1854. Assemblyman 1855. Moved to San Francisco 1862. Founded bank in San Jose 1863. State senator from Santa Clara County 1866–1867.

John A. Lancaster — He and wife operated Virginia House (1852) and the Union Hotel (1853–1855). Proprietor of livery stables in the 1850s and 1860s and manager of National Exchange Hotel in 1864. Town trustee. Captain of Nevada City Light Guard 1865.

John Randolph McConnell — Practiced law in Nevada City 1850–1861. District attorney 1851–1852. California Attorney General 1854–1855. Ran for governor in 1861 and was defeated by Leland Stanford. Practiced law in Nevada 1861–1866 before returning to Nevada City in 1866. Moved to Los Angeles in 1870s, which he represented in the state assembly in 1875–1876.

Thomas B. McFarland — Mined at Selby Flat, north of the city, in the 1850s. Practiced law at Nevada City 1854–1870. State assembly 1856; district court judge 1862–1869. Moved to Sacramento and served as Register of U.S. Land Office. Member of 1878 California Constitutional Convention. Superior court judge 1883–1886; state supreme court justice 1887–1902.

Charles Marsh — Prospected Deer Creek July 1849. County surveyor 1851–1855. Member of first county board of supervisors 1855–1857. Voters accepted his proposal to build a new water system for Nevada City in 1860. In December 1860 he and Theodore Judah and Daniel Strong created the Central Pacific Railroad Company; in 1861 he was elected to the board of directors, along with Stanford, Hopkins, Crocker and Huntington, et al. President of Nevada Library Association 1864. (His home on Nevada Street is owned by the Nevada County Historical Society.)

Martin Luther Marsh — Miner and carpenter at Kentucky Flat, French Corral and Nevada City in 1852. Bought interest in sash factory and sawmill in 1859 and became a very successful lumberman. County supervisor 1873–1876. Officer of Trinity Episcopal Church 1874. Officer of Nevada City Benevolent Society.

Edward Eddy Matteson — Located the Merrifield Mine in 1851 with Charles Marsh and Dr. McIntyre. In 1853 he conceived the original concepts for modern hydraulic mining. In 1860 he invented a water-powered wheel that could remove trash from flumes, as well as a hydraulic derrick that lifted and moved heavy objects from streams.

John T. Morgan — Blacksmith, miner. Arrived at Nevada City in 1853, moved to North San Juan in 1859, returned in 1874. County assessor 1871–1874. Founding officer of Citizens Bank, eventually its president.

Charles William Mulford — Opened book and stationery store 1850. First local Wells Fargo agent 1852. Established private bank 1855–1862. One of first officers of Trinity Episcopal Church.

Addison Cook Niles — Practiced law at Nevada City 1855–1872 and 1880–1883. Justice of the peace 1855–1856; county judge 1863–1871; state supreme court justice 1872–1878.

James J. Ott —Swiss-born chemist and metallurgist, cousin of John Sutter. Came to Nevada City in 1852. Developed chlorinating process to recover gold from sulphurets. His assay of ore sample from Comstock silver mine set off rush to Virginia City in 1859. Part owner of Oriental quartz mill 1863–1865. Town trustee 1866.

Ianthus Jerome Rolfe — Part owner of *Nevada Democrat* 1854–1863. President Nevada Library Association 1859. Part owner of *Nevada Daily Gazette* 1864–1865. President of Eureka Hose Company No. 2 in 1880.

Tallman H. Rolfe — Printer at *Nevada Journal* 1851. Part owner of *Young America* 1853. Justice of the peace 1853. Part owner and sometime editor of the *Nevada Democrat* 1854–1863. County supervisor 1860–1862. Went to Nevada state and edited the *White Pine Gazette* 1864–1865. Returned to Nevada City and was justice of the peace in 1871.

Aaron A. Sargent — Part owner and sometime editor of the *Nevada Journal* 1851–1856. District attorney 1855–1857. Town trustee 1855–1856. Charter member Oustomah Lodge #16, IOOF (1853) and Nevada Library Association (1858). Partner of George F. Jacobs in the Quaker Hill Mine. Congressman 1862–1872. Introduced bill that authorized and funded transcontinental railroad in 1862. Served in U.S. Senate 1873–1879 and introduced Susan B. Anthony's bill to give women the right to vote. Minister to Germany 1882–1884. Practiced law in San Francisco 1885–1887.

Ellen S. Clark Sargent — Wife of Aaron. Founded the Nevada County Woman Suffrage Association in 1869 and worked closely with Susan B. Anthony (who sometimes lived with the Sargent family). In 1888 she and Phoebe Apperson Hearst founded the Century Club at San Francisco, where women could meet to hear notable speakers of the day and discuss political and social issues—a radical concept then.

Lorenzo Sawyer — Practiced law in Nevada City 1850–1853 before moving to San Francisco to serve as city attorney. He was judge of the 12th district at Redwood City in 1862–1863, California supreme court justice in 1864, and chief justice 1867–1869. In 1870 he became the first U.S. circuit court judge for the west coast. His ruling ("Sawyer Decision") in 1884 essentially stopped hydraulic mining.

Father John Shanahan — Established St. Peter and St. Paul's Catholic church in Nevada City in 1852 at Coyote and Washington streets. Poor health led to his reassignment to St. Peter's church in San Francisco, where he served as assistant priest.

Niles Searls — Practiced law 1850–1864, 1869–1885, and 1890–1893 at Nevada City. Edited the *Young America* and its successor, the *Nevada Democrat* 1853–1854. District attorney 1854; district court judge 1855-1861; state senator 1877–1878; California supreme court commissioner 1885–1887 and 1893–1899; chief justice of the state supreme court 1887–1888. In 1892 he represented the California Miners Association in Washington, D.C., successfully arguing for partial restoration of hydraulic mining. (His law office on Church Street is owned by the Nevada County Historical Society.)

William Morris Stewart — Arrived in 1850 and was Charles Marsh's partner in building the Grizzly water ditch in 1851. Practiced law 1852–1857 at Nevada City. District attorney 1852–1854; California attorney general pro tem 1854. Moved practice to Downieville (1857) and Genoa (1860). Member of Nevada Territorial Legislature and Constitutional Convention. Beginning 1865 he served 5 terms as U.S. senator from Nevada.

Joshua N. Turner — Lumberman 1850–1862. In May 1850 he used lumber from a single tree to build Nevada City's first frame hotel. Designated by legislature in 1851 to oversee first elections in Nevada County. Assemblyman 1852. Town trustee 1854. Moved to Oroville and elected to Assembly from Butte County in 1870.

Edwin G. Waite — Miner 1851. Assemblyman 1855; state senator 1856. Editor and part owner of *Nevada Journal* sporadically 1855–1861. Editor of *Morning Transcript* 1861–1864. County treasurer 1862–1863.First treasurer of Nevada Benevolent Society in 1867. Political writer for *San Francisco Times, Sacramento Union,* and *Overland Monthly* 1868–1889. U.S. Naval Officer of San Francisco (1873–1881; California secretary of state 1891–1894.

Rev. James H. Warren — First minister of Nevada City Congregational Church 1851–1858. Moved to San Francisco in 1858 to edit *The Pacific,* a religious periodical. Participated in 1860 dedication of "Founders Rock" on the future U.C. campus at Berkeley. Pacific Coast Superintendent of American Missionary Society 1869–1894.

Isaac P. Williamson — Storekeeper and auctioneer 1850–1857. Part owner of saloon 1858. Amos Laird's partner at the "Lost Hill" hydraulic mine 1855–1870. Co-manager of Union Hotel 1864. Active in early efforts to establish a fire department between 1852 and 1856. President of Protection Hook and Ladder Co. No. 1 in 1864. Town trustee 1867.

Early Fraternal Organizations, Benevolent and Mutual Aid Societies

Masonic Bodies

Nevada Lodge #13, F&AM

In early April 1850 the Grand Lodge of Wisconsin authorized the formation of Lafayette Lodge #29, Nevada City's first Masonic Lodge. On April 20, 1850, the Grand Lodge of California was instituted and on May 6, 1851, authorized a charter for Nevada Lodge #13, which displaced Lafayette Lodge #29.

The fires of 1851 and 1856 destroyed the Lodge's first two buildings (on Coyote Street and Broad Street, respectively). The current lodge building on the southeast corner of North Pine and Commercial streets was built in 1864. John Riggs Crandall was first Master of the Lodge.

E. K. Kane #72, F&AM

A charter was granted E. K. Kane Lodge on April 2, 1855. Charles Seymour was first Master. The charter was surrendered on December 1, 1858, and the membership merged with Nevada Lodge #13.

York Rite:

An appendant Masonic body and the oldest of the Masonic Rites, York Rite embodies three organizations: Royal Arch Masons, Knights Templar, and Cryptic Masons (the latter not constituted until early in the 20th century).

Royal Arch: The Grand Chapter issued a dispensation for a Nevada Chapter on April 30, 1855. Thomas Caswell was the first High Priest.

Nevada Commandery #6, Knights Templar: Founded in the 11th Century, Knights Templar were originally laymen who protected Christians travelling to Jerusalem. Modernly, they provide money for medical research and educational assistance. A dispensation was issued by the Grand Commander to institute a Commandery in Nevada City on November 3, 1858; a charter was granted on July 21, 1859. The first officers were Thomas Caswell, Charles Marsh, Samuel Boring, Niles Searls, John B. Bope, Christopher Reis, William Ferguson and Orange Dibble. In 1865

Thomas Caswell, Isaac Williamson, Martin Luther Marsh, Thomas Hawley, Addison Niles, Aaron Sargent, S. R. Eddy, James H. Helm, Allen Chapman and Joseph B. Gray reorganized the lodge.

Order of Eastern Star:
An adoptive rite of Freemasonry, with teachings based on the Bible and with charitable and benevolent objectives, the Order was founded by Robert Morris, who published his first ritual in 1849–1850. Robert McCoy thereafter published a ritual in 1867, based on Morris' work, and the first Grand Chapter was organized in Michigan that same year. William Schyler Moses introduced the Order in California on May 10, 1869, in San Francisco. It is the largest fraternity in the world that allows both men and women to be members.

Sponsored by Nevada Lodge #13 F&AM, Evangeline Chapter #9 in Nevada City was chartered in August 1873. The first elected officers were Emily Rolfe (Worthy Matron), Thomas Caswell (Worthy Patron), Lucy Caldwell, Zerlene Goldsmith, Cecelia Boardman, Clara Barton and Alice Locklin.

Independent Order of Odd Fellows (IOOF)

Founded for purposes that included giving to those in need and pursuing projects for the benefit of all mankind, The first IOOF lodge in California was founded in San Francisco in September 1849. Oustamah Lodge #16 in Nevada City was chartered on November 4, 1853.

The first lodge hall, rented space in the Hamlet Davis building at Pine and Broad Streets, was destroyed in the 1856 fire. The second hall, built on the south side of lower Broad Street (site of the current National Hotel parking lot) was destroyed in the 1863 fire. The current lodge building, on the south side of Broad Street, was constructed in 1873, on the site of the second Masonic Hall. The first officers were Aaron Sargent, L. B. Austin, James B. Van Hagan, H. D. King and B. F. Ferrell.

Esther Rebekah Lodge #9
Schuyler Colfax introduced the Degree of Rebekah in 1851. This first fraternal organization for women in the United States was first chartered in Iowa in December 1868. The Nevada City Order was chartered March 2, 1872. The first officers were Ann E. Webber, Mrs. Harriet F. Lakenan, Emma Quick, Mrs. M. B. Townsend, Virginia P. Smith and Mrs. Mary J. Sims.

Sons of Temperance

The objective of the order was to shield its members from the evils of intemperance, to elevate character and to "assist in the suppression of drink traffic." Also acting as a mutual aid society, the organization was formed in New York in 1842. Introduced in California about 1854, the organization by 1855 had 15 divisions in Nevada County. Nevada Division #17 and the Nevada Temple were both located in Nevada City. In 1860 the Order was supplanted by the Independent Order of Good Templars, which organization admitted women. There were, however, no lodges in Nevada City.

Improved Order of Red Men

Originally called The Sons of Liberty, this fraternity was founded in 1765. With identities concealed, members worked to "establish freedom and forge liberty in the colonies." Protesting a tea tax imposed by England, in 1773 members disguised as Mohawk Indians dumped 342 chests of English tea into Boston Harbor.

After the Revolutionary War, the organization's name was changed to the Order of Red Men. Their rituals and objectives were patterned after the Masonic organization.

Wyoming Tribe #49 was instituted January 30, 1874 in Nevada City. The first officers were T. C. Plunkett, Samuel Clutter, Ianthus J. Rolfe, Erastus Bond, J. C. Dean, George M. Hughes, G. von Schmittburg, D. Marsh and H. C. McKelvey. Meetings were held at the Odd Fellows Hall.

Independent Champions of the Red Cross

Originating on the west coast in 1873, the fraternity promoted temperance and provided literary, musical and other cultural entertainment for members. Both men and women were eligible for membership.

Manzanita Encampment #43 was organized in Nevada City on March 27, 1875. The first officers were Edward H. Gaylord, Samuel Clutter, J. C. Rich, T. C. Plunkett, W. F. Evans, G. W. Smith, L. J. Blundell, William Holmes and W. C. Bradley. The membership, at times as many as 80, met at Odd Fellows Hall.

Knights of Pythias

Nineteenth century scholar Justis Rathbone was inspired to create the Knights of Pythias after seeing *The Story of Damon and Pythias* by the Irish playwright John Bynam. Impressed with the play's concepts advocating peace and goodwill among men, Rathbone wrote the rituals and statutes for the proposed organization. The first lodge was instituted in Washington D.C. in February 1864.

Milo Lodge #48 was formed in Nevada City on November 1, 1878, with 34 charter members. The first officers were George M. Hughes, J. W. Robinson, J. A. Rapp, Oscar Maltman, J. G. Hartwell, George O. Gray, Joseph D. Fleming, Walter D. Vinton, A. R. Lord and H. S. Welch. Meetings were held at the Masonic Temple.

Order of Caucasians

Founded in Sacramento in March 1879, the Order's mission was "for the protection and elevation of Caucasian labor, the promotion of social and intellectual intercourse among its members, and the establishment of a system of general philanthropy, charity and benevolence, providing for the sick and distressed, the widow and orphan, for the decent interment of deceased members . . . ."

The Nevada Camp #73 was organized in Nevada City on August 9, 1879. The first officers were E. B. Ebaugh, L. Ragan, F. G. Guild, W. White, F. G. Richmond, Paul Richards, J. P. Ebaugh and J. G. Gillman. Meetings were held at the Odd Fellows Hall.

Nevada Benevolent Society

Organized in Nevada City January 22, 1867 for the purpose of "aiding the deserving poor, such as are not reached by other methods of charity." The first officers were George K. Farquhar, Edward F. Spence, Edwin F. Bean and Edwin G. Waite. The first directors were G. von Schmittburg, A. Goldsmith, Jonathan Clark and James Monro.

Ancient Order of United Workmen

This Order was organized as a mutual benefit and insurance society that provided sickness, accident and death benefits to members or survivors. Nevada Lodge #52 was instituted September 17, 1878, with 23 charter members. The first officers were C. W. Cross, Edward H. Gaylord, James D. White, Charles E. Mulloy, George Robinson, George Gaylord, R. D. Carter, W. H. Crawford,

W. H. Smith and Henry Grover. Meetings were held at the Odd Fellows Hall.

Ancient Jewish Order, Kesher Shel Barsel

On April 5, 1855, the Nevada Hebrew Society was organized for charity, benefits and endowments. In 1863 the Nevada Hebrew Benevolent Society was formed from the predecessor group; in 1873, the Society merged with North Star Lodge #120 AJOKSB. The first officers were A. Goldsmith, J. Greenwald, L. Jacobs and E. Goldsmith. Meetings were held at the Masonic Temple.

Benevolent and Protective Order of Elks

The Benevolent and Protective Order of Elks (BPOE) was originally a group calling itself the Jolly Corks, organized by Charles Algernon Sidney Vivian, an English entertainer who migrated to New York City in 1867. Composed primarily of theatrical entertainers, the social club gravitated toward charitable purposes and reconstituted itself as the BPOE on January 16, 1868. New York Lodge #1 was chartered by New York State on March 10, 1871, and granted authority to establish lodges throughout the United States.

Nevada City BPOE Lodge #518 was formed October 14, 1899, with Edward Myers Preston installed as the first Exalted Ruler. The membership met weekly at the Odd Fellows Hall on Broad Street until purchasing an 1860s building at the southwest corner of Pine and Commercial streets. A second-story addition for use as the lodge hall was completed in January 1913 and occupied two months later.

Destroyed by fire on July 14, 1914, the lodge was immediately rebuilt and occupied by January 1, 1915. The facility remained the home of the Elks until August 4, 1996, when its new building on State Highway 49 was dedicated.

The former Elks building at Pine and Commercial streets was destroyed by fire on March 20, 2002.

Appendix C

Nevada City Gold Rush Era Churches

Nondenominational Christian

Organized: Summer 1850
Location: Building of shakes and poles constructed on upper Broad
  Street
Original membership: Unknown
First pastors: Rev. Lamden, Rev. R. R. Dunlap, Rev. C. A. Leaman

First Methodist Church *
(formerly Methodist Episcopal Church)

Organized: October 1850
Location: Upper Broad Street building dedicated summer 1851.
Relocated to present Broad Street location in 1852. Building de-
  stroyed by 1856 fire. New building destroyed by 1863 fire.
Present church built 1864.
Original Membership: 20
First Pastor: Rev. C. A. Leaman

Methodist Episcopal and
Methodist Episcopal South
churches before the 1856 fire.

Methodist Episcopal Church South

Organized: Fall 1851
Location: Broad Street. Church building completed November 13,
  1851; destroyed by 1856 fire. Church not rebuilt and organization
  was abandoned.
Original Membership: Unknown
First Pastor: Rev. John F. Blythe

Congregational/Presbyterian Church

Organized: April 1851

Location: First services held at Dramatic Hall. Church building on at Church and Main streets occupied September 1851; destroyed by 1856 fire. New building dedicated January 1858; destroyed by 1863 fire. New building dedicated April 10, 1864. The church disbanded in 1914 when Rev. Josiah Sims moved to San Francisco after 42 years as its pastor.

Original Membership: 21

First Pastor: Rev. James H. Warren

Congregational church (1856) and St. Canice Catholic church (1857).

St. Canice Church *

(formerly St. Peter and St. Paul's Church)

Organized: 1852

Location: First church built at Coyote and Washington Streets 1857, destroyed by 1863 fire. Church rebuilt at same location in 1864 and renamed St. Canice Church.

Original Membership: Unknown

First Pastor: Father John Shanahan

Nevada City Baptist Church *

Organized: August 28, 1853

Location: Services held at Dramatic Hall in 1854. First church built at Pine and Spring Streets in 1854. Building destroyed by fire in 1856 and rebuilt in 1857. In mid-1950s, building still stood but was converted to secular purpose. At that time, congregation purchased former Congregational church building on Main Street (built in 1864) and rehabilitated it to its present condition.

Original Membership: 29

First Pastors: Rev. Myron Newell, Rev. J. M. Winn, Rev. O. B. Stone

Left: Baptist church in 1856. Right: Congregational brick church in 1900; built in 1864, it now is home to Nevada City Baptists.

Trinity Episcopal Church *

Organized: April 1854
Location: First services held in Congregational Church. First church
   built and destroyed in 1863.
Present building on Nevada Street completed 1874.
Original Membership: 40
First Pastor: Rev. William H. Hill

Trinity Episcopal Church, located on the approximate site of Caldwell's "Upper Store," was built in 1874.

African Methodist Episcopal Church

Organized: 1858
Location: Pine Street church building dedicated September 18, 1864;
   collapsed March 1865.
Original Membership: 10
First Pastor: Rev. Robert Tyler

* Currently active

Appendix D

Nevada City Cemeteries

Historic Cemeteries

Pioneer Cemetery

The Methodist Church established the oldest cemetery in Nevada City in 1851 on the church's original site on West Broad Street. The two and one-half acre cemetery is now owned by the city of Nevada City. Among the pioneers either buried or with monuments at Pioneer are Congressman and Senator Aaron Sargent, John Sutter's son, William Alphonse Sutter, and horticulturist Felix Gillet. The cemetery is no longer used as a burial site.

St. Canice Cemetery

Records of the early history of this Catholic cemetery, located on West Broad Street adjacent to Pioneer cemetery, are non-existent, generally believed to have been destroyed in one of Nevada City's early destructive fires. The cemetery is presumed to have been established sometime after the church was organized in 1856. The earliest burial, as reflected by an examination of the readable headstones, was that of Patrick McInerney who died in 1878.

Nevada City Jewish Cemetery

The Nevada City Hebrew Society was formed in 1854 and soon thereafter purchased land for a cemetery, located at the end of King Hiram Drive (private road), off Searls Avenue. The cemetery has 29 observable headstones. The first known burial was that of Carolyn Himes who died in 1856. The last burial was in 1890. Title to the cemetery is held in trust by the Judah L. Magnes Museum's Commission for the Preservation of Pioneer Jewish Cemeteries and Landmarks.

Nevada City Chinese Cemetery

The first Chinese in the area were buried in Chinese sections of regular cemeteries. However, the Chinese custom of subsequent exhumation for shipment of remains to China was not palatable to local citizens and Chinese cemeteries became a necessity.

The Nevada City Chinese cemetery was built on 1.3 acres of Bureau of Land Management land (without permission) and was in use by (and probably before) 1891. Located near the present Northern Queen Motel on Sacramento Street, the cemetery has been privately preserved as a historical site by the Ramey family. It is believed that all remains had been removed from the cemetery by 1930.

Pine Grove Cemetery

Located on the south side of Red Dog Road just outside city limits, the ten-acre parcel was purchased in 1860 by William C. Groves, an undertaker and cabinet maker. The county surveyor thereafter divided the parcel into plots. Groves was elected county coroner in 1863 and in 1864 he built a sidewalk from downtown Nevada City to the cemetery.

Sections within the cemetery are owned primarily by local fraternal organizations, most notably Nevada Lodge #13, F & A.M. and Oustomah Lodge #6, I.O.O.F. Also located within the cemetery is a section devoted to local Civil War veterans.

Hooper and Weaver Mortuaries own sections within the cemetery not otherwise owned. The only remaining burial plots within the cemetery are owned by Nevada Lodge #13, F & A.M. Influential pioneers buried in the Masonic section of the cemetery include Judge Niles Searls and lumberman Martin Luther Marsh.

Modern Cemeteries

On the north side of Red Dog Road, across from Pine Grove Cemetery is another I.O.O.F. cemetery, established when the fraternity ran out of plots in Pine Grove. It is currently used for burials.

Adjacent to the newer I.O.O.F. cemetery is the Forest View Cemetery, established in the mid-1950s by Nevada City entrepreneur Eddie Ferrano.

Ferrano also established Sierra Lawn Cemetery on the grounds of Hooper and Weaver Mortuary on Hollow Way. Hooper and Weaver purchased Sierra Lawn and Forest View from Ferrano in the mid-1990s. Both cemeteries are in current use.

Appendix E

Selected Nevada City Landmarks

Listed by map numbers:

1. **Indian Medicine Stone** — East Broad and North Pine streets
2. **American Hill Diggings** — West Broad Street, near Chief Kelly Dr.
3. **Pioneer Cemetery** — Upper end of West Broad Street
4. **Nathaniel P. Brown House** — 528 East Broad Street
5. **Englebright House** — 524 East Broad Street
6. **545 Main Street: The Spence, Niles and Searls Families** — 545 Main Street
7. **Baruh Home** — 516 Main Street
8. **Saint Canice Catholic Church** — Washington and Coyote streets
9. **Old Brick Gothic Church** — Main and Church streets
10. **Nevada City Firehouse No. 1** — 214 Main Street
11. **First Brick Building in Nevada City** — 212 Church Street
12. **Searls Law Office** — 214 Church Street
13. **Doris Foley Library of Historical Research** — 211 North Pine St.
14. **Aaron Sargent House** — 449 Broad Street
15. **Nevada City Methodist Church** —Broad and Mill streets
16. **Nevada City Firehouse No. 2** — Broad Street (across from Nevada Theatre)
17. **Nevada Theatre** — 401 Broad Street
18. **Nevada City Hall** — 317 Broad Street
19. **Miners Foundry** — 325 Spring Street
20. **Nevada County Traction Company** — Pine and Broad streets
21. **Kidd and Knox Building** — NE corner Pine and Broad streets
22. **Flagg Building** — SE corner Broad and Pine streets
23. **Powell House** — SE corner Pine and Spring streets
24. **National Exchange Hotel** — 211 Broad Street
25. **Ladies of The Evening** — National Hotel parking lot
26. **Calanan Park Monitor and Drill Core** — Broad and Union streets
27. **South Yuba Canal Office, Ott Assay Office, Five- Stamp Mill, Pelton Water Wheel, and Wells Fargo Building Site** — Foot of Main Street

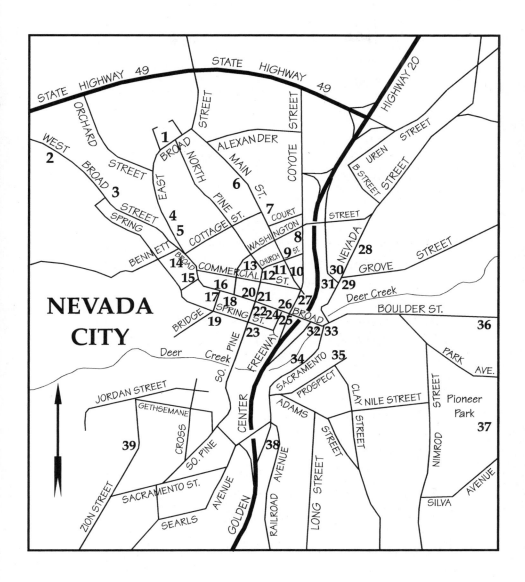

Location map for selected Nevada City landmarks.

28. **Howard Naffziger Home** — 216 Nevada Street

29. **Colley House** — 128 Nevada Street

30. **Trinity Episcopal Church and Site of Caldwell's Upper Store** — Nevada and High streets

31. **Charles Marsh House** — 123 Nevada Street

32. **Plaza Grocery** — 101 Broad Street

33. **Nevada Brewery** — Sacramento Street near Plaza

34. **Allen Chapman House** — 227 Sacramento Street

35. **The Red Castle** — 109 Prospect Street

36. **Martin Luther Marsh House** — 254 Boulder Street

37. **Isabel Hefelfinger Wagon Shed** — Pioneer Park

38. **Nevada County Narrow Gauge Railroad** — Railroad Avenue

39. **William Morris Stewart House** — 416 Zion Street

Listed alphabetically:

Bibliography

Ashley, Mabel. *Gold Rush Theater in Nevada City, California*. Master's thesis, Dept. of Speech and Drama, Stanford University, 1967.

Best, Gerald M. *Nevada County Narrow Gauge*. Berkeley: Howell-North, 1965.

Browne, Juanita Kennedy. *A Tale of Two Cities and a Train*. Nevada City: Nevada County Historical Society, 1987.

Calhoon, F. D. *A Self-Guided Tour of the Grass Valley: Nevada City Mine Sites*. Sacramento: Cal-Con Publishers, .1991.

Carlson, Anne. *Tahoe National Forest Cultural Resources Overview*. Part II: Ethnography, 1986.

Comstock, David. *Gold Diggers and Camp Followers 1845–1851*. Grass Valley: Comstock Bonanza Press, 1982.

———. *Brides of the Gold Rush 1851–1859*. Grass Valley: Comstock Bonanza Press, 1987.

———. *Greenbacks and Copperheads 1859–1869*. Grass Valley: Comstock Bonanza Press, 1995.

Hagaman, Wallace. *The Chinese Cemetery at Nevada City, California, and Chinese Burial Customs During the Gold Rush*. Nevada City: The Cowboy Press, 1998.

Jackson, Joseph Henry. *Anybody's Gold: The Story of California's Mining Towns*. San Francisco: Chronicle Books, 1970.

Janicot, Michel. *The Ladies of the Night: A Short History of Prostitution in Nevada County*. Nevada City: Mountain House Books, 1996.

Koon, Helen Wickham. *Gold Rush Performers: A Biographical Dictionary of Actors, Singers, Dancers, Musicians, Circus Performers and Minstrel Players in America's Far West, 1848–1869*. Jefferson, NC: McFarland and Company, 1994.

Lardner, W. B., and M. J. Brock. *History of Placer and Nevada Counties, California*. Los Angeles: Historic Record Company, 1924.

Lescohier, Roger. *The Cornish Pump in the California Gold Mines*. Nevada City: Roger Lescohier, 1992.

———. *Lester Pelton and the Pelton Water Wheel*. Nevada City: Roger Lescohier, 1992.

———. *The Stamp Mill for the Recovery of Gold from Hard Rock*. Nevada City: Roger Lescohier, n.d.

———. *More Gold from the Same Ore*. Nevada City: Roger Lescohier, 1992.

Mann, Ralph. *After the Gold Rush: Society in Grass Valley and Nevada City, California 1849–1870.* Stanford: Stanford University Press, 1992.

May, Philip Ross. *Origins of Hydraulic Mining in California.* Oakland: The Holmes Book Company, 1970.

Morris, Susan. *A Traveler's Guide to Pioneer Jewish Cemeteries of the California Gold Rush.* Berkeley: Commission for the Preservation of Pioneer Jewish Cemeteries and Landmarks, Judah L. Magnes Museum, 1996.

Nevada County Landmarks Commission. *Catalog of Historical Landmarks and Dedicated Sites in Nevada County, California.* Grass Valley: Comstock Bonanza Press, 1999.

Prisk, W. F. Jr., J. E. Poindestre and Samuel Butler. *1895 Pictorial History of Nevada County.* (Reissue of *Nevada County Mining Review* and *Grass Valley and Vicinity*.) Grass Valley: Comstock Bonanza Press, 2000.

Sheafer, Silvia Anne. *Chinese and the Gold Rush.* Glendale, CA: Journal Publications, 1998.

Thorne, Tanis C. *The Campoodie of Nevada City: The Story of a Rancheria.* Nevada City: Sansoucci Publications, 2000.

Wells, Harry L., et al. *History of Nevada County, California.* Oakland: Thompson and West, 1880.

Suggested Further Reading

Browne, Juanita Kennedy. *Nuggets of Nevada County History.* Nevada City: Nevada County Historical Society, 1983.

Hagaman, Wallace. *Chinese Temples of Nevada City and Grass Valley 1868–1938.* Nevada City: The Cowboy Press, 2001.

Lescohier, Roger. *The Miners Foundry.* Nevada City: Roger Lescohier, 1998.

Thorne, Tanis C. *Indians of Nevada City in 1854.* Nevada City: Sansoucci Press, 1993.

Index

Edwards, John, 8
Eighth Judicial District, 9
Elevator Flouring Mill, 36
Elks Lodge #518, 47, 76
Empire Gambling Saloon, 49, 50
Empire Livery Stable, 8
Empire Mine, 17, 63, 66
England, 74
Esther Rebekah Lodge #9, 73
Eureka Hose Company #1, 45-46
Evangeline Chapter #9, 73
Evans, William F., 74
Ewer, Warren B., 38, 39, 41, 67

Farquhar, George K., 75
Felt, Alney O., 8
Ferguson, William, 72
Ferrano, Eddie, 81
Ferrell, B. F., 73
Fleming, Joseph D., 75
Fogeli, Casper, 36
Forest View Cemetery, 81
Foster, John S., 8
Foster's Bar, 42
Fourth-of-July parade, 66
France, 53
Fraser River strike, 34
Fraternal orders: Caucasians, 75;
  Champions of the Red Cross, 74;
  Eastern Star, 73; Elks, 47, 76; Good
  Templars, 74; Hebrew, 35, 76, 80;
  Knights of Pythias, 74–75; Masons,
  72–73, 75–76, 81; Odd Fellows, 73–
  76, 81; Red Men, 74; Nevada
  Benevolent Society, 75; Sons of Lib-
  erty, 74; Sons of Temperance, 74;
  United Workmen, 75; Rebekah, 73
French Corral, 25
French Saloon, 57
Frisbie, Lyman P., 51, 68
Frisbie's Concert Hall, 51
Frisbie's Theater, 10

Gault, Alexander, 60
Gault bridge, 60

Gaylord, Edward H., 74, 75
Gaylord, George C., 75
Gem Photo Theatre, 54
Georgia, 13
Gillet, Felix, 68, 80
Gillman, J. G., 75
Gold Run (Creek), 6, 36, 44
Golden Center Freeway, 23, 48, 58,
  64, 66
Golden Days (stage play), 55
Goldsmith, A., 75, 76
Goldsmith, E., 76
Goldsmith, Zerlene, 73
Gottschalk, Louis Moreau, 53
Grand Lodge of California F&AM, 72
Grass Valley National (newspaper), 39
Grass Valley Telegraph (newspaper), 39
Grass Valley, Calif., 16, 17, 26, 32, 50,
  52, 59, 61, 66
Gray, George O., 75
Gray, J. B., 43
Gray, Joseph B., 73
Greenhorn Creek, 28
Greenwald, J., 76
Gregory, A. B., 8, 68
Grover, Henry, 76
Groves, William C., 81
Guild, F. G., 75
"Gyrator breaker," 16

Hallidie, Andrew, 59
Hartwell, J. G., 75
Hawaii, 31
Hawley, Thomas P., 68, 73
Hayes, Catherine "Kate," 53
Helm, James Harvey, 8, 26, 73
Henry, J. B., 36
Herzinger, Henry L., 43
Hieronimus, Simon, 36
Hill, Rev. William H., 79
Himes, Carolyn, 80
Hoit, Moses F., 8, 68
Holmes, William, 37, 74
Hooper and Weaver Mortuaries, 81
Hopkins, Mark, 6, 25

About the Author

Orval Bronson is a resident of Nevada City and is a member and former director-at-large of the Nevada County Historical Society. His first book, *Burning Brightly: John Steinbeck on Stage,* was published in 2000.